# OAKWATCH

# OAKWATCH

*A seasonal guide to the natural history
in and around the oak tree*

## Jim Flegg

*Illustrated by Dianne Breeze*

Pelham Books
London

First published in Great Britain by
Pelham Books Ltd
44 Bedford Square
London WC1B 3DP
1985

Flegg, Jim
Oakwatch: a seasonal guide to the natural history in and around the oak tree.
1. Oak—Great Britain    2. Habitat (Ecology)
I. Title    II. Breeze, Dianne
574.5'2642        QK495.F14


ISBN 0 7207 1619 5


Filmset in Ehrhardt by BAS Printers Limited, Great Britain
Illustration reproduction by Chelmer Litho, Great Britain
Printed and bound by Arnoldo Mondadori, Italy

*For Caroline,*
*with love*

# CONTENTS

The advent of winter; problems of survival; goldcrest activity; feeding techniques of tit flocks: thrush food; value of roosts; long-eared owl ecology; woodpigeons and pest control; mild spells; problems of snowfall; thrush weight changes; identifying tracks; dormouse survival; flourishing grey squirrels; acorns and their uses; heron activity.

Plant growth resumes; mistle thrush, the early songster; song learning in the chaffinch; lichens on the trunk; the woodpeckers; floral spectacular; the oak buds burst; bullfinch damage; bats in the oakwood; migrant birds appear; chiff-chaff and willow warbler; the cuckoo saga; colonial nesters – herons and rooks.

Harvest mites; specialist oakwood plants; studying insects; moths, caterpillars and colours – to camouflage or to frighten?; oakwood butterflies and their food; insect predators and prey; blood-sucking flies; stag beetles and others; leaf miners; treecreeper and nuthatch ecology; breeding problems of tits; birds of prey; importance of defoliating caterpillars; summer visitors; turtle dove and nightingale; western oakwood birds; oddities and rarities; woodcock – the odd wader out; nematode recolonization after the Ice Ages; slugs and snails; birds in moult.

Plant survival from year to year; seed dispersal adaptations; birds and autumn fruits; weight changes in migrant and resident birds; migration; bird mortality; redpoll and goldfinch, seed eaters; jay and oak, a symbiosis; oak apples and other galls; gall wasp life-cycles; autumn fungus forays; stinkhorn life-cycle; fungi helpful and harmful; fallen trees as a habitat; the thieving magpie; the vociferous shrews; deer in oakwoods, natural and introduced; rutting and delayed implantation; contrasting lives of fox and badger; fieldmice and voles – prey for all; autumn colours; brown birds – dunnock, wren and tawny owl; sparrowhawk – supreme woodland hunter.

# PREFACE

This is a book about an oak tree and its life and times with the various other plants and animals that live on it, in it or near it through the changing seasons of the year, all of them in some way influenced by its majestic presence. It is not 'any old oak', but then nor (for the sake of completeness) can it sensibly be just one single oak tree in particular. Even in an area as small, geographically speaking, as Britain and Ireland, there are quite dramatic differences in climate and soil that influence the oaks of the area and their inhabitants. Thus 'the oak' of this book is an average enough specimen, mature, some 80 feet (24 m) high with a trunk circumference a yard above the base of about 15 feet (4.5 m), widening to an amazing 30 feet (9 m) at ground level round its root buttresses. It is growing in an oakwood somewhere in lowland England, on a slightly heavy clay-loam soil. It bears no little similarity to one that I see from my house every day, a tree that has played a substantial part in this account of the natural history of the oak.

The wealth of plant and animal life in and around a mature oak tree is such that no book could ever hope to encompass mention of *all* the possible other 'characters'. If the 'supporting cast' for the oak in this book seems exaggeratedly large and over-idealized, this point should be brought back to mind. Oak trees, in oakwoods, are an extraordinarily rich and varied habitat, and provide one of the best locations for field studies that any naturalist could wish for, whether it be with a butterfly net, a beating tray, a hand lens (or even a microscope), a flora or binoculars.

Jim Flegg

# ACKNOWLEDGMENTS

The idea for *Oakwatch* arose in discussions with Richard Douglas-Boyd, who like myself lives in and loves a fifteenth-century oak-framed hall house set among more modern oaks on the Weald of Kent. His enthusiasm encouraged me to draw on my experiences with oaks in various parts of Britain and to merge with them, in several areas where my own knowledge was scanty, some of the detailed knowledge of experts in the fauna and flora associated with this species of tree. Individual references would be impossibly complex to cite, but one book has been an invaluable source: it is *The British Oak*, the proceedings of a conference at the University of Sussex in 1973, published in 1974 by the organizers, the Botanical Society of the British Isles, and edited by Drs M. G. Morris and F. H. Perring. The authors of the twenty-seven contributions to this work each provide further reference sources relevant to their topic: I am grateful to them all. Fortunately, Caroline my wife and our sons Matthew and William share my enthusiasm for natural history, and show this in their tolerance. Caroline, too, has been an invaluable help in getting 'things' straight (be they spelling, grammar or whether or not something has already been mentioned or omitted) and in deciphering and typing much-amended manuscripts.

The illustrator, Dianne Breeze, would like to thank the Merseyside County Museum for providing specimens, with a special acknowledgment to Miss C. Fisher and Mr S. Judd for their help.

*AUTHOR'S NOTE*
The units of measurement expressed in this book are those which are in common usage. Where helpful, dual units, i.e. metric and imperial, will be found side by side. The main exception to this is in the expression of bird weights where the gram is the standard unit used.

# INTRODUCTION

The oak tree is familiar to us all, its massive four-square appearance dominating the rural view, its distinctive leaves and acorns often used as design motifs, its timber prime amongst native hardwoods for the manufacture of furniture. The acorns were used in the Middle Ages as pig food, and for centuries oak was the structural basis of all ships of war and many domestic dwellings, from the cottage to the manor house. 'Hearts of oak are our ships, hearts of oak are our men . . .': music and folklore are rich in oak references and myths, folk medicine likewise, while other chemical by-products – for example, tannin for leather treatment – play their part in our everyday lives. But what of the life of the oak tree? If it survives a hazardous beginning, it may endure for centuries. Its bark and foliage often carry more types of insect that any other tree, and trunk and branches likewise support record numbers of lichens. Such richness is reflected too in the numbers of mammals and birds that are associated in some way or another with the oak, perhaps living in the shelter of its branches, or perhaps feeding off it or its associated wealth of life.

Not only is the oak familiar, but it has become part of our tradition, held in esteem and affection. A Scotsman, William Boutcher, writing on forest timber, called the oak 'this noble tree, the monarch of the woods, the boast and bulwark of the British nation'. Only recently, though, has the richness of its natural history been a major reason for our appreciation of the oak. For many centuries its popularity rested on its usefulness in the various ways listed above, the most important of which was as a source of timber. This was of a size, strength and durability to make it the major structural building material until iron and steel came on the scene. It came in lengths, and with branch angles, that lent themselves to both galleon and house building. One has only to think of the size of major mediaeval buildings with timber-supported roofs – cathedrals, for example – to appreciate just what enduring structural properties oak has and how well they were exploited by early craftsmen. Oliver Rackham (writing in *The English Oak*) listed some of the oak timbers in such buildings: Norwich Cathedral main roof, for example, contains almost 700 oaks with a basal diameter of about 18 inches (45 cm), and the main roof of King's College Chapel, in Cambridge, is made of over 500 oaks, about one quarter of them over 2 feet (60 cm) in diameter. In contrast, a hall house built in about 1500 (an upper middle-class dwelling of which many examples still exist) contains about 300 oak trees, some as small as 6 inches (15 cm) in diameter, though most between 6 and 18 inches (15–45 cm), and with only the major crossbeams coming from trees exceeding 18 inches (45 cm). Normally the timbers used would have only been squared off, not sawn lengthways, hence the range of sizes employed.

In some ways this enthusiasm for and pride in oaks in the British Isles seems strange, for the native oaks that we esteem so highly are just two species, among the most northerly of representatives of a vast genus of trees coming from warm-temperate or even tropical climates. All are in the genus *Quercus*, which by botanical standards is a large one containing some 500 different species. Moving south from Britain and around the globe, southern Europe has around twelve species, but Mexico, in the 'New World', boasts about 200! Eastwards from Britain, other oak species are to be found throughout Europe and Asia to the Far East in China and Japan, and south-east through Malaysia to the Philippines.

There is no doubt, however, from a study of fossil remains and pollen grains in peat bogs, that deciduous oak forest has for thousands of years been the natural climax vegetation – if you like, the all-embracing ancestral forest type – of Britain and Ireland. Our two species, *Quercus robur*, the pedunculate, stalked or common oak, and *Quercus petraea*, the sessile oak, are not the easiest to distinguish, even though found in an area that has long held civilized man and which cradled the science of taxonomy.

Broadly speaking, the pedunculate oak, though very widespread, is most typical of the deeper, slightly heavier (and thus water-retentive) soils of southern England and the Midlands, growing with a wide variety of shrubs (like hazel, elder and hawthorn) and small plants (like drifts of bluebells or wood anemones). Sessile oakwoods are more characteristic of the rugged, hilly scenery created by the older rocks in western England, Wales, Scotland and Ireland, where they grow with a wide variety of other plants around them, bracken and bramble being dominant. But sessile oaks do also occur in the south and east where the soils are sufficiently acid. On lighter soils, like gravels and sands, in southern England, both species of oak are found, growing over typical heathland plants like heathers and gorse. In this setting, and elsewhere, hybrids between the two oaks occur that further confuse the identification issue.

In simple terms, the pedunculate oak (as its name implies, for 'penduncle' means 'stalk) carries its female flowers – which after fertilization grow into acorns – on stalks an inch or more long, carried in turn on the twigs. The leaves are of a typical oak-leaf shape, even to the extent of having a couple of lobes pointing 'backwards' where the leaf blade (or lamina) joins the leaf stalk (or petiole). In contrast, the sessile oak has no such lobes, the lamina fanning out smoothly from the petiole, and carries its flowers (and acorns) without stalks at the bases of the leaf stalks and attached directly to the main twigs – 'sessile', freely translated, meaning 'seated'. Hybrids show a varied mixture of their parental characters.

There is more to it than this, however, as the pedunculate oak was in the past of considerably greater importance to man: it produced a larger and more regular acorn crop for pig food, and, as it was usually of more substantial stature, it produced bigger and better constructional timbers, which in addition tended to have natural branch angles suitable for forming the crucks (angled beams or braces) in timber-framed buildings.

Other oaks have been introduced to Britain as ornamental trees, over thirty species in total. Of these, among the commonest is the evergreen or holm oak, *Quercus ilex*, whose dark green upper leaf surfaces contrast with their silvery undersides. The Turkey oak, *Quercus cerris*, is another widespread introduction; it has a spiky acorn 'cup' which hosts many of the gall wasps, seemingly with little ill-effect. The red oak, *Quercus borealis*, from the New World, planted like the other introductions for its ornamental value, is rather less common than the native species; its leaves, which are much larger, have triangular points rather than semicircular lobes along their edge.

Of all the acorns produced by the oak during its life, the vast majority go to feed other living things. In autumn, the occasional acorn survives the onslaught of gall wasp and weevil, jay and woodpigeon, and falls to the ground to be buried in soil and leaf litter. It may be, even, that the jay has helped by carrying the acorn some distance and then burying it safely as an emergency food source, cached but not subsequently used. If this acorn then survives the winter searches of starving-hungry squirrels and small rodents, it germinates in the spring. The shell splits, and a tiny two-leaved shoot, whose leaves are already recognizable as those of an oak, pushes upwards, growing on the food stored in the acorn, while a root system develops and penetrates the soil.

If all goes well, the root establishes and the small oak tree grows to a few inches in that first summer. More often than not, however, it is eaten by grazing animals like rabbits or deer, trampled, overshaded by other plants, killed by drought, or mortally injured by insect or fungus attack, to be seen no more. If it survives, at a year old it might be 1 foot (30 cm) tall (at best) with slightly improving chances of success, although many hazards, natural and man-made, remain. After ten years, a good sapling might be 10 feet (3 m) or more high, and on its way – barring accidents – to meeting the poet Dryden's suggested criteria for 'the monarch oak, the patriach of trees'. Dryden was probably not too far adrift from a natural time scale when he suggested that the oak spent a century growing to maturity, a second century secure and supreme in its maturity, and a third

15

century in a gradual decline to ultimate death.

The oak that forms the centrepiece of what follows is probably at the end of Dryden's idealized second phase: mature, still very robust and secure, but missing the odd branch as a result of storms and with the occasional rotting limb or tell-tale bracket fungus on its trunk indicating its age, but at the same time providing yet more habitats for its already richly varied accompanying wildlife.

# WINTER

NLY rarely does winter descend with a sudden severity reminiscent of the clang of a prison door closing behind the cell's occupant. Normally, the onset of winter is well heralded through the autumn, warning those plants and animals that overwinter in a quiescent state. Winter is predominantly a grey season: the oaks are skeletal in their grey bark, the woodland floor beneath them grey-brown with fallen leaves, and the skies above grey more often than not.

Through the autumn, day lengths have steadily decreased until, just prior to Christmas, they are at their minimum, before gradually but agonizingly slowly lengthening again as spring approaches. Correspondingly, the nights that have to be survived are long, and the frosts, rain, sleet and snow (and, just as important, high winds) of the season add to the difficulties of keeping alive by increasing the 'chill factor' or by effectively reducing the daylight hours. To survive overnight, the warm-blooded active creatures of the wood must find and eat enough during the brief period of daylight both to keep them going *and* to put aside some as an 'internal store', to be metabolized during the hours of darkness to keep body heat at the necessary level.

The oaks themselves are bare by midwinter, although some will have retained their browning leaves much longer than others, and one or two may keep their old foliage until the spring – an ancestral trait, this, caused by their failure to produce a complete abscission layer sealing off the area where leaf and stem adjoin. Even though they have lost the protection of the leaf bases, the buds, with leaves and flowers in embryo form, are well guarded by the waxy brown bud-scales, impermeable to wind and weather. The general drabness is relieved by the continuing presence of the algae and lichens and by the fact that some of these – particularly those flourishing greenly where rainwater courses down branches and the trunk – may be even more apparent than during the summer.

The bark of the oak is deeply fissured and cracked, far more so, for example, than ash or beech, and on a par with elm. Thus for small creatures – especially arthropods – it provides a useful shelter. Many more spiders, for instance, are found on oak than on, say, birch or Scots pine, and it is thought that this is because of its accommodating bark. Some spiders, like *Clubonia brevipes*, overwinter in the cracks in oak bark. For those insects that overwinter as eggs – and the number of both species and individuals involved is huge – the twigs of the tree are especially important. Although some adult insects actually penetrate the wood, sometimes deeply, to lay their eggs, most lay on the surface, usually selecting crevices, cracks, leaf scars or little corky pimples on the bark, called lenticels, for protection: the winter moth, whose caterpillars are so important to the oakwood web of life in early summer, is one of these. Those insects which overwinter as larvae usually do so on the twigs or among the buds. Small moth larvae will spin for themselves surprisingly robust cocoons (or hibernacula) of silken threads tucked away in a bud cluster.

Beneath a mature oak there is little to be seen but the deep leaf litter, but elsewhere in the wood can be seen clumps of the peculiar butcher's broom with its assegai-shaped 'leaves' (actually flattened stems capable of carrying on the life-supporting process of photosynthesis). In the centre of each flattened stem (called a cladode) can be seen a tiny thorn-like leaf, with the diminutive flower in its axil in summer now transformed to a red berry. Presumably once used in bunches as a besom to sweep sawdust from butchers' floors, these plants are now more at risk from gypsies who pick them for their evergreen qualities and ability to survive under a layer of

*Goldcrests*

Christmas 'glitter' as household ornaments. Such plants as this, and the ivy so often to be seen both on the ground and on the trunks of trees, have a cell-sap functioning chemically as an 'antifreeze' which protects them from damage by severe weather. Under the lesser oaks, and in the clearings, winter has collapsed the grasses and bracken to a tangled matting protecting the base of the plants, and the tall proud plants like teazels and thistles have been reduced to frost-fringed rosettes of leaves hugging the ground.

For many animals, however, life must go on and survival is paramount. They may not hibernate and have no sheltered overwintering stage as egg or pupa, and so are dependent on what the oak provides. For them winter is no 'dead' season but one of feverish activity if they are to stay alive. At this time the food and shelter that the oak provides may be of the utmost importance. The ecological and environmental 'value' of woodland is often calculated on the number of breeding creatures it supports: perhaps this is a false premise.

In October and November, oakwoods may sometimes swarm (there is no other appropriate word for it) with goldcrests, particularly after a series of mild winters when their numbers are high. These little birds, weighing about 5 grams (almost six of them to the old-fashioned ounce), the smallest in Britain, are always on the move, wings flickering, and piping their tiny shrill call. From twig to twig, bud to bud they hop – first upright, then upside down. However many times these feeding movements are watched – often at very close quarters, sometimes too close to use binoculars – it remains difficult to answer the question of how they land upside down. Do they fly alongside right way up and then do a sideways roll to perch feet upwards, or do they approach at low level and then 'loop the loop', perching at the top of the loop? At this time the bulk of their food is the eggs that various insects have secreted in the cracks in the bark – the goldcrests use their needle-fine beaks to get at these. Close to, the crest on an actively feeding bird is seen as a thin, dark-bordered, pale yellow line down the centre of the crown; but should one male trespass too closely on the feeding space demanded by another, the head feathers are fluffed out and the crest raised as in the courtship display. Then the amount of yellow feathering can be seen, and the deep flame bases to the feathers show, startlingly, to best effect.

It is always difficult to grasp the fact that these delicate little birds have reached this country after crossing the North Sea. Surely something so weak and fragile just could not survive the length of the journey, let alone the buffeting of the frequently wet and windy autumn weather.

Occasionally, the goldcrest flocks are accompanied by a similar-sized and even more handsome relative, the firecrest. There is little difference in the colour of the crest – despite what the names suggest, the females of both species have yellow crests while the males of both have flame-coloured crests with a greater or lesser degree of yellow tips. Otherwise the firecrest can be quickly distinguished by the black and white horizontal stripes across its face above and below the eye, and by the golden bronze mantle (back feathers) – much more striking than the goldcrest's plainer olive. Perhaps it is because they are such small birds that the mantle feathers seem to have a superfine quality all their own.

November is the time that the tit flocks contain the greatest variety – the huge parties of August, September and October are overwhelmingly composed of blue and great tits, and the very small flocks of January and February are also predominantly composed of these two species. In November, other species are involved, including goldcrests, treecreepers and nuthatches, wrens and chaffinches, and the occasional chiff-chaff, perhaps a late migrant or, nowadays increasingly likely, a bird hoping to overwinter in Britain. Coal tits are frequently seen – sometimes some Continental birds with their very much richer colouring are recognizable amongst them. Whole flocks of long-tailed tits may appear: these delightful birds have very strong family ties, and call incessantly to keep in contact with their relatives. They are surprisingly mobile considering their cumbersome long tails, short rounded wings and apparently feeble flight, and these family parties may range over several miles, crossing from one block of woodland to another using the farmland hedgerows as a sheltered 'highway'. The two drabbest tits may also be involved – marsh and willow – as always, difficult to distinguish other than by their calls: the 'dee-dee-dee' or 'chay-chay-chay' of the willow and the ringing and explosive 'pit-chu' of the marsh.

It is interesting to watch how the various species differ in their reactions to tit flocks. The flocks, and their hangers-on, seem to swirl through the trees almost like falling autumn leaves blown by sudden gusts of wind. There are pauses, when few birds are actually in the air, which indicate when a particularly suitable oak has been found, rich in food, and then a sudden flurry of wings and calls as the mob moves away. The great and blue tits may wander over a considerable area – roaming like gypsies – but some of the other birds are far more conservative. Treecreepers and wrens, for example, although they will probably join in the activity of a group when it is in their vicinity and the excitement of so many other food-seeking birds nearby is at its peak, will lose enthusiasm as the party heads towards the boundary of their winter 'home range', which may be quite small. But as some drop out of the swirling horde, others in adjacent territories are drawn in to participate in their turn.

*Nuthatch*

Just what is the benefit of this mass approach is open to debate: many pairs of eyes seeking food at many levels obviously gives a better chance of finding a really good oak for feeding, and clearly those same eyes will provide an effective early-warning system should a predator approach. But then why does the party move on so quickly to a fresh oak, only to return again a few hours or days later? Clearly, although the feeding was good, for some reason the opportunity was not fully exploited at the time.

A flock of birds descending on an oak provides the chance to watch *how* the tree is exploited by a group of mixed species and different feeding habits. On the ground beneath the oak, turning over the leaf litter and probing beneath the bark and in the soft timber of any fallen decaying branches or twigs, will be the chaffinches and great tits and sometimes the nuthatches if acorns are to be found. The great tit may also search low on the bole and trunk of the tree, while the nuthatch, should it find an acorn that has not been worked over by a squirrel or a vole, will fly up with it in its beak to a favourite crevice in the bark. Here, using the crevice as a combination anvil and vice, it will hammer open the acorn and devour the nutritious kernel within.

The treecreepers meanwhile will be circling the trunk and major branches, long hooked claws holding them fast to the rough bark. Unlike the nuthatches, which move with equal facility head-up or head-down and do not use their tails as a prop, the treecreepers have a tail (similar to that of members of the woodpecker family) with specially stout central feathers. They always move head uppermost, lying back on the tail and using it like a shooting stick. The crevices in oak bark are particularly deep on the trunk (compared with the branches and twigs), and of the usual woodland birds only the treecreeper has a beak long enough, yet fine-pointed enough, to probe sufficiently deeply to remove the insect eggs or larvae secreted there. For their size treecreepers have relatively large eyes and this too may be an adaptation helping them to locate their prey in the gloom of the crevices.

So to the outermost branches and twigs. Here the smaller tits once again subdivide the available feeding resources, and thus reduce the pressure on any one location. Keeping a tally on the time spent in various feeding stations on the oak will show that the marsh and willow tits spend most on relatively substantial branches, with the marsh tit occasionally feeding on the ground as an alternative, while the willow sometimes resorts higher, to the twigs. In contrast, blue, long-tailed and coal tits spend most time on the outermost twigs, where their supreme agility at feeding in any position serves them well. It is difficult to imagine how they can effectively see to hunt out minute insect eggs, hanging upside down and swaying in the breeze, but obviously they manage to as every line of their body portrays intense concentration while they peer and probe amongst the bud clusters. Once found, the insect eggs themselves are so minute that again the imagination has to work overtime to comprehend their being collected and eaten fast enough to supply the energy so obviously used in hunting them out.

Jays, too, are at their most obvious at this time of year. When they flop away from the oak and across the wood or out on to the surrounding farmland, they look unusually heavy-headed. They will probably soon be back, sometimes calling harshly. The reason for their big-headedness is apparent once they can be seen with binoculars: they are carrying acorns. These they will pick up from the leaf litter or pluck from the branches before taking them out and burying them, apparently at random, in nearby fields. Apart from the scattering of food to be found later by chance (it seems they have no 'intelligent' way of finding them again) by jays or other birds or animals, this does ensure some spreading of oak trees when a few of the acorns germinate!

In the early days of winter, the oakwood will see a tremendous influx of members of the thrush family and starlings, whose prime aim in life, it seems, is to gobble up as quickly as possible the berries on the various shrubs in the undergrowth – predominant among them haws and wild rose hips. Many birds just do not need to leave the wood during the day. Plentiful food is available, and new arrivals like redwings, with their thin seep call and rufous-feathered 'armpits', or fieldfares, with their harsh chuckle, can be observed at close quarters, for many of them have as yet little familiarity with man. Surely these two must be amongst the most handsome of our birds – especially the fieldfare with the rich subtlety of its greys, chestnuts and blacks.

Superficially it may appear that the thrushes are running a severe risk of eliminating their winter food supply before they need to, because worms and other soil animals are still plentiful and easily found. It could be, however, that it is more important for the bird to be in the right condition to face the problems of winter. If it starts off with suitable reserves, a minimal daily food intake will suffice to keep it alive, whereas if it waits until daily food, fat reserves and fatty insulation layers are all needed *at the same time*, the chances of successfully meeting these demands from available food are poor, especially in the shorter daylight hours. More than any other factor, the shortness of the day imposes the greatest threat: not only is adequate food vital for a bird's normal functions and health, but in winter most birds have an insulating 'jacket' of body fat under the skin to maintain, together with fat reserves to tide them over any periods of unusually severe weather. To this should be added the fact that food produced during the summer in the form of seeds, nuts and berries has

*Robin*

already been exploited for some months by adult birds and their most recent offspring, making each mouthful the more difficult to find and the more vulnerable to competition.

Thus from the late daybreak right through to dusk, the majority of the birds of the wood will be feeding actively – some, like the dunnocks and tits, remaining within its confines; others needing to make forays to the surrounding farmland or, in times of greatest stress, to the gardens of homes in a nearby village. In such circumstances it is important for the birds that they lose as little heat as possible – hence the winter appearance of the robin, fluffed out to retain an extra-thick 'string-vest' layer of insulating air close to its body.

At the end of the summer most small birds moult many or all of their feathers. Adult birds and the young of the year all shed their badly-worn, thin, body feathers and these are replaced by a new set, more robust and more weatherproof on the outside and with a much fluffier, thicker down at the base. It is this down that insulates them against the cold, but it too is subject to wear and tear and gradually breaks down during the winter, so that by the time the weather is growing warmer the bird is not slowly cooking inside its 'thermal underwear'.

A bird's energy requirements – drawing on the precious stores of body fat – are not much reduced overnight and will be increased by the cold in winter. The night is a long one and temperatures may be considerably lower than in the daytime, so the best available shelter is sought out for roosting and squabbles over favoured perches may be just as violent, and just as important, as those taking place over a worm or a crab-apple fragment during the hours of light. Exposure to a slightly colder draught of air right through the night may make a great deal of difference to a small bird.

Thus the oak itself, and the hawthorn, blackthorn, bramble and gorse elsewhere in the wood, serve their purpose. In late afternoon, small groups of birds begin to gather, twittering and chattering. The finches and thrushes usually move straight into the roost, but starlings may gather at a series of pre-roost spots before taking off to the main roosting area. The take-off moment, when tens of thousands and sometimes hundreds of thousands of starlings are involved, is preceded by a sudden silence – almost painfully oppressive in comparison with the previous racket – before the roar of wings surges out.

Midwinter is the time to find long-eared owls roosting in the oak – during the daylight hours, as most of their hunting is done in the fading light of evening or at night-time. Not every year will they be seen, as most, if not all, are likely to be immigrants from Scandinavia, driven south and west either by the severity of the winter in the countries where they breed or

*ong-eared owl hunting at dusk*

because their numbers
are so high that the available
winter food resources just cannot
support them. With so many small
birds roosting in the wood around
the oak, food is not so difficult to
come by after dark for the owls at
least. With a little luck, one or two
of the group that spends the winter in the
wood will be out hunting before the light has failed completely,
and the astonishing silence of an owl's flight (due to a specialized
feather design and the velvety feather surface) can be appreciated.

During the day, the owls roost more or less communally, as is their
custom. A cautious approach – quite difficult to achieve – will reveal them
perched close to the main trunk. If undisturbed, the birds will be 'at ease'
– fluffed up and looking like tawny owls, but even in this 'plump' condition
exceedingly easy to overlook. One small sound, any indication that they
have been seen, and they freeze, first closing their feathers and slimming
right down to the thickness of neighbouring branches. In this tight-
feathered condition, sitting bolt upright, their cryptic colouration – a
mixture of black, white and rich browns – serves them admirably for

25

camouflage, and often the first sign of their presence is a silent, heart-stopping departure from right beside you. When they do fly, their agility is amazing: they are quite big birds, with a wingspan approaching 3 feet (90 cm), but they can twist through the branches and twigs without a sound – apparently just as easily as a woodcock.

Late in the afternoon long-eared owls can be quite eerie birds to watch for, other than in the breeding season, they make little noise, and the movements of any intruder passing quietly through the roosting area are followed by startlingly fierce orange eyes. Only the owl's head moves (it can turn through more than 360°) and the structure of the head epitomizes the bird. The long feather tufts that give the bird its name have no hearing function, but the true ears are most remarkable: they are very large and also asymmetrical, a system that allows detection of very slight sounds and a precise location of their source. Experiments have shown that this superb hearing facility enables long-eared owls to hunt successfully in total darkness.

Sometimes two or more owls will work co-operatively in hunting a finch roost. One flies conspicuously down on one side of a line of bushes while another lurks quietly, sparrowhawk-like, before making a dash at some of the birds disturbed by its fellow. Looking at the pellets (or castings of fur, feathers and bone) that the owls regurgitate after a meal reveals much about their food requirements; ironically, as bird rings also are indigestible, it shows something of the fate of ringed birds too. Birds may form quite a large element of the winter food of long-eared owls and it is surprising to find rings from hole-roosting birds, like the tits, among those from finches and sparrows. It is difficult to conjecture how these tits are caught!

In Britain in the breeding season, the long-eared is the typical conifer woodland owl, but this preference is not an absolute one and every few years a pair will linger on in the oakwood into the spring, when their regularly spaced, low-pitched 'oo-oo-oo-' hooting adds an unusual dimension to the late-winter bird song. On occasion they nest in an oak, perhaps using as a base an old woodpigeon's nest deep in the ivy at the angle of a massive side branch and the trunk, or even a magpie's nest, disused since the first occupants reared their young in it the previous summer. On the nest they sit very low, and are just as difficult to spot as when they are roosting.

Long-eared owls often decapitate larger prey, and the accumulations of pellets beneath regularly-used roosting branches may often also have the odd head, usually of a blackbird or similar-sized thrush, lying among them. Occasionally, though, the signs of a kill are far more conspicuous. Sometimes a trail of feathers will lead to a fox kill – perhaps a pheasant, but more often a woodpigeon. The soft, white, down feathers that insulate the pigeon in winter are scattered over an extraordinary distance from the corpse – and seem so copious that it is difficult to imagine how they were ever all crammed on to the live bird. Presumably these victims were roosting low enough to be snapped up on the jump by the fox, but on occasion (and indeed perhaps frequently) it may be a case of the fox 'tidying up' behind a farmer. With a considerable acreage of tempting brassicas in their care, now that cereals have displaced many of the clover-rich leys, farmers have to work hard to guard their crops and the winter day is regularly punctuated with shots as they pursue hungry marauding pigeons. Obviously many birds are just 'winged' and limp, injured, to the wood for shelter. They cannot attain the high, safe roosting spots in the oak and in many cases are quickly put out of their misery by foxes.

*Fox with woodpigeon*

Despite the amount of work that has been put into the study of woodpigeons by the Ministry of Agriculture, all tending to show that (as in many bird populations) winter weather, food shortage and disease combine to reduce the population naturally by the spring to the level of the previous year, farmers are understandably rather difficult to dissuade from forceful protection of their crops. They remain unconvinced that the level of control that their attempted slaughter achieves is only sufficient to ensure that there is enough food for all the remaining pigeons, and that their major ally, starvation, is thus hardly allowed to become effective. It is interesting to reflect, too, that the headlong pursuit of fashion and the debatable grail of increased profit margins has caused farmers to abandon clover pastures – the pigeon's preferred winter diet – and to a large extent bring this plague upon themselves.

February is a month of change for the oak: a mild, open winter may be brought to an abrupt halt by a few inches of snow and sub-zero temperatures, emphasizing what winters *can* be like, or alternatively there may be a spell of quiet, fine weather with surprising warmth in the sun at midday, and with pale rose sunsets.

Should the latter be the case, it is astonishing how quickly the mood of incipient spring grips both the woodland plants and animals. The rusty brown bracken from the previous summer that has since autumn impeded progress by tripping the unwary seems suddenly to have flattened. Beneath the oak, bluebell shoots appear, pushing aside the leaf litter and making 2 or 3 inches' (5–7.5 cm) growth in the month. Early dog's mercury may even flower there too – very discreetly, for the tiny green-petalled rosettes are objects of beauty only under a magnifying glass. In the more sheltered spots elsewhere in the wood, soft adventurous shoots spring from the underground elder stems – rapidly burnt off in the merest hint of a frost – and in the clearings a few flickers of gorse bloom at the start of the month may have turned into a yellow blaze as March approaches.

Mild weather also provokes a fairly substantial amount of song. The mistle thrushes, perched high on the topmost branches of the oak, no matter how strong the wind, are now hard at it, and may have built a nest – a bulky structure of moss and leaves (and, all too often today, streamers of torn polythene bags) set in the angle of a branch, or atop a thick branch at an elbow. Mistle thrushes sound their best on milder days as the sky mellows towards sunset. Song thrushes, although less numerous than blackbirds, at this time of year outdo them in the dusk chorus, and only towards the end of the month does the rich fluid song of the blackbird oust the more stilted, repetitive phraseology of the song thrush. Taking time off from foraging with other tits, treecreepers and goldcrests, male great tits

begin stridently to stake their territorial claims in the wood, often centred
here, as in many other woodlands, on a nestbox – an artificial nesting site
provided by a conservation enthusiast or by a forester keen on encouraging
insect-eating birds. The 'tee-chah tee-chah tee-chah' is often the precursor
of the other disyllabic song in the oak, that of the chiff-chaff.

How different this story is if, as not irregularly happens, February turns
really savage and several inches of snow cover the ground. To the birds this
picturesque covering must present a totally unappealing aspect. The ground
on which so many of them feed has vanished, and should there have been
a glazing frost, or a thaw followed by a snap freeze, the buds and twigs on
the oak are inaccessible even to the flocks of tits and goldcrests, encased
in an impenetrable but glass-clear ice coating.

The first signs of impending trouble are to be seen overhead – lapwings
and skylarks, many probably coming from the Continent, are passing
westwards moving towards warmer areas on our oceanic seaboard.
Woodpigeons, too, are on the move. Relatively few of these will be
Continental, to judge from the recoveries of ringed birds, but mostly local
inhabitants looking for fields of kale or Brussels sprouts where the strength
and height of the plants has broken the snow cover and exposed some
eatable greenery. Over such fields the fusillade of shots increases in tempo,
and flocks of increasingly hungry birds wheel across the sky.

In the wood, the thicker canopy of the oak (and the very dense
hawthorns) keeps some ground free of snow, although some hawthorns may
collapse completely under the weight of the accumulated snow. Into the
snow-free area crowd all the thrushes that have previously used the wood
only as an overnight shelter, leaving each morning to forage in the fields,
sometimes up to several miles away. They mostly come in from the
Continent during the autumn as part of their regular migration pattern, and
now join in the search, and competition, for food with the birds that spend
their whole life as residents in or near the oak. Sometimes dozens of
blackbirds, fieldfares, redwings and song thrushes will work systematically
in crescentic waves through the leaf litter, turning over everything time after
time, and making, just by their rustling, a noise like a herd of foraging pigs!
When a small invertebrate animal is found, a tremendous battle may
develop if the unfortunate discoverer does not devour its find immediately
– the energy that is wasted in squabbles of this nature, with birds leaping
high in the air and feathers regularly flying can only contribute to their
problems. Such disputes can also arise simply when one bird encroaches
on the much-reduced-by-circumstances hunting area of another.

In these conditions, overnight losses of weight – caused by the
metabolism of stored fat which maintains body warmth and functions – may

approach ten per cent of total body weight, and a bird such as a blackbird can generally only manage a week of really lean days before reaching a 'point of no return'. It is for survival in just these conditions that so many birds put on weight before or during the winter. A striking example of the role that man can play is offered by comparing 'town' blackbirds – helped over hardship by benevolent housewives with ample scraps – with their less fortunate country cousins. A good midwinter weight for a healthy woodland blackbird is about 130 grams, compared with a midsummer weight of about 100 grams. Luxury-fed town birds may maintain a 140-gram level right through a cold snap, while the birds in the oakwood rapidly lose weight, falling perhaps to about 100 grams after a week and to 80 grams or below after two weeks of snow cover. At around the 80-gram mark most are pathetically feeble, and it seems that when this milestone is reached many blackbirds can no longer survive for corpses become increasingly obvious. Redwings suffer even more severely after a week, when their normal 60–70 grams falls to about 40, and many can be seen literally dying on their feet, incapable even of flight. Even though the thinking naturalist must accept this levelling of numbers as an essential for healthy populations of a variety of species – for 'safety's sake' most species over-produce young during the breeding season, and the oldest and least fit, physically or otherwise, perish during the period before the next breeding season – it remains hard to remember the general principles of evolution and survival when confronted with the actual mortality.

Even when snow does not accompany lengthy severe frosts, there are problems for the thrushes in breaking through the frozen crust of soil beneath the oak to get at the small invertebrate animals (like slugs, beetle larvae and worms) for food. Part of the problem is a downwards migration of these animals to slightly warmer soil, but at least as important is the mechanical difficulty. In years when severe frost extends over two or three weeks, it is the thrushes with the shortest beaks that suffer first – redwings, then song thrushes, fieldfares and lastly blackbirds and mistle thrushes.

In these conditions, while the thrushes suffer, the tits tend to seek their own salvation along the lines of the urban blackbirds. Shortly after the snowfall begins, all will start moving towards the nearest village (and presumably towards well-stocked bird tables) from all parts of the wood – clearly getting out the quickest way. This departure is a regular and fascinating feature at the onset of harsh weather, but although the feeding may be better near human habitation and survival apparently more reliable, other previously unfaced hazards occur; some birds may be caught by domestic cats making the best of unexpectedly easy hunting, or fall foul of fast-moving traffic.

A white Christmas – or indeed a period of snowfall at any time during the winter – is surely the ideal time for the tracker to interpret what is happening. Follow the bold tracks of a pheasant, punched through the thin crust on the snow, and identify it as male from the tell-tale thin line where the long tail has been allowed to drag in the snow. The spots where it has stopped to forage are only too obvious – a black-brown scar where a bucketful of leaf litter and snow has been churned up. Sooner or later, surely, it must take off – and the impression of the wing feathers in the snow at the spot shows more clearly than any other way the lift that the apparently ineffectual short round wings can produce to get the heavy bird off the ground in one flap. The primaries (longer feathers on the edge of the wing), when spread out, are each clearly defined, and the impression is pushed perhaps 2 inches (5 cm) deep into the snow.

Here and there are the 'two together, two in line' tracks of rabbits of all sizes, and the even pawprints of a fox. Fox paws, while basically dog-like, are more diamond-shaped, and in snow a trotting fox leaves its prints in a near-dead-straight line, evenly spaced, showing how balanced and beautifully poised its movements are. These are among the best conditions to get a good view of a fox. Keep downwind of it, quiet and still, and it may come quite close. Fox numbers are currently so high in both town and country that the foxes seem to be becoming quite nonchalant in the presence of humans, going about their business seemingly content with the world. On encountering man, instead of bolting, they now coolly turn and retrace their steps, just as if a rather important engagement elsewhere had suddenly been remembered.

When there is no snow, the muddy paths in early morning will show even the most inexperienced tracker the volume of traffic that has passed in the night. At this time of year, not only are the foxes most mobile, but they are also at their most vocal. In the evening, the vixen's scream is answered by the dog fox's sharp bark. After dark, this produces a sound that remains spine-chilling to the naturalist, no matter how many times he or she has encountered it. There is nothing in wildlife more human-sounding, nor more blood-curdling, than the scream of a vixen – and even the strongest of stomachs must pause to take a grip on itself.

A closer look at the paths in February shows a different sort of foot pattern altogether – likened best to the sort of print a fairly small human baby would leave. There is a clearly marked oblong 'sole', and along its leading narrow edge are arranged five neat little toes. Sometimes a track like this can be followed for hundreds of yards, and traced back into a hawthorn or elder thicket beneath the oaks. Here, in a mild February, other signs of badgers – for badger tracks they are – are apparent in the form of grass and leaves, turfed out of the badgers' underground set as elderly and unwanted bed litter in the first 'spring clean' of the year. As the years pass, what the badgers have dug for themselves become fairly considerable earthworks, with a number of entrances, sometimes many square yards in extent. The now-trampled-down mounds of soil from their excavations are often 2 or 3 feet (60–80 cm) high, and as the set entrances are normally in gullies about a foot (30 cm) deep, the going nearby can be treacherous – for man, at least.

In among the rabbit tracks may be found signs of the smudged passage of squirrels – not surprisingly, with such short legs they try to keep in the oak as much as possible when the ground is snow-covered, but when they must descend, they try to get the nasty business over quickly, scurrying on splayed legs through a cloud of snow with tails held high and out of the way. Albino grey squirrels are not uncommon, and a sudden sighting of the all-white shape (quite large, taking the fluffed tail into consideration) can produce quite a jolt as it ghosts quietly away along a branch in late afternoon.

The foxes are not the only nonchalant winter mammals by the oak. After a while, a period of quiet, motionless watching will be broken by mysterious scufflings beneath the deep leaf litter. Sooner or later, flickering whiskers appear, followed by a long narrow snout, and ultimately by a shrew – to judge from the length of its tail, a pygmy shrew. Shrews, as insect or other small-animal eaters, must of course keep feeding right through the winter to keep their energy level high enough to survive. Not for them the luxury of short periods of hibernation through bouts of poor weather such as those the mice and voles can indulge in. In a mild winter, voles and fieldmice will be active throughout, while the main hibernating animals, the bats (usually choosing a sheltered hollow branch or cleft in a lightning-struck

*Pygmy shrew*

oak trunk), the dormouse (in much smaller cavities and occasionally in nestboxes, but still well above ground level) and the hedgehog (there is usually one to be found in a 'nest' of leaves and grass tucked a few inches underground in a cavity beneath one of the oak's major roots) will always have prolonged quiescent periods.

The dormice – the native common dormouse and the introduced edible or fat dormouse, grey rather than chestnut in colour and supposedly brought in by the Romans because of its gastronomic qualities – are the most complete hibernaters of British mammals. Consequently the quality and quantity of the food available to them in late autumn and early winter is of the utmost importance, as it determines the amount of fat that they can store and thus their winter survival potential. Although the oak shelters the occasional common dormouse, these get most of their food from the shrub layer – particularly favouring hazel nuts. Elsewhere in the country – particularly in the few areas of southern central England where it is common – the edible dormouse does depend more heavily on the oak for its food. It is bigger and more agile than its relative, and much more at home climbing in the canopy, and so the acorns that it can reach and consume quickly build up an adequate fat store for the winter.

Intriguingly, both dormice will sometimes use a nestbox as a hibernation site, and here they can be seen best (and with least disturbance to their deep slumber – it is important to their survival that this is not broken). Curled into a ball, tail draped over nose and face, they seem quite dead, so cool is their temperature and so low and irregular are their heartbeats and breathing movements. Nearer spring, an early circuit of the nestboxes to clear out any remaining old nests will sometimes reveal these overwinter tenants. The common dormouse always seems drowsy and slow-moving, and rarely if ever makes any noise. In marked contrast, the edible dormouse can come to with alacrity, and will freely give vent to its annoyance by literally bristling with rage and producing a scolding chatter that sounds just like an electric sewing machine attempting to stitch together sheets of tin!

Conspicuous up in the leafless canopy of the oak at this time is the winter drey of a grey squirrel. Lodged securely in a substantial fork, this ball of broken-off twigs, many still holding their leaves from the autumn, provides its resident with a reasonably warm, waterproof and windproof lair to help it survive the winter. The grey squirrel is an introduced animal, its true home being the deciduous woodland of North America. Before it was released in Britain in 1876, it seems unlikely that oakwoods would have been much exploited by the other member of its family, the truly native red squirrel, which shows a strong preference for coniferous woodland. Sadly, the grey squirrel has flourished too well and is now both numerous and widespread over much of England and Wales, but less common in the Borders and in Scotland, and in Ireland. As it is much more catholic in its choice of food, the grey squirrel has also colonized coniferous woodland and, being larger and more aggressive (and for these and other reasons more successful) than its cousin, has displaced the red squirrel from much of England and Wales.

In North America, the grey squirrel is held in high esteem by sportsmen as a shooting quarry, completely at odds with the situation in Britain, where it is often called, disparagingly, the 'tree rat' and is notorious amongst foresters as a pest because of the damage it does to hardwood trees when it strips off the bark. This feeding habit seems to have developed on this side of the Atlantic, and in severe cases will result in the death, by girdling, of major branches or sometimes the whole tree. The grey squirrel is even unpopular with woodland naturalists and conservationists because of the heavy toll it takes during the breeding season of small birds' eggs and young.

Despite its conspicuous bark eating, it is the acorns that are of most importance to the grey squirrel in winter. These may be eaten while still attached in the canopy, and with its agility and sharp claws the grey squirrel has little difficulty in reaching the most way-out of them, sometimes using its tail as a counterpoise as it stretches, at maximum reach, to obtain a particularly tempting mouthful. Other acorns are eaten on the ground after they have fallen, and many are taken away and buried – a food cache against hard times during the winter.

34

*Grey squirrel*

Many of these are subsequently recovered – apparently located by scent – and dug up from their shallow hiding places and eaten.

An interesting evolutionary contrast can here be drawn between the grey squirrel and the wild boar – sadly no longer a denizen of British oakwoods. These two mammals depend heavily on acorns to help them survive winter's harshness, both putting on fat in autumn. The present-day domestic pig's ability to fatten up quickly is doubtless derived from an ancestral ability to gorge on the autumn glut of acorns. Because they are large and ferocious in the face of adversity, wild boars have few predators other than man. Thus they can afford to gorge and become extremely fat in autumn at the expense of a great reduction in their mobility and agility. The grey squirrel, on the other hand, is vulnerable to a range of predators as varied as stoats and foxes, cats and dogs, owls and buzzards, and therefore must at all costs retain its speed and climbing capability; talents readily displayed when the oak's resident squirrel is disturbed on the ground in midwinter and rapidly reaches its refuge in the higher branches, its feet seeming hardly to touch the bark as it goes. The squirrel stores most of its harvest *externally*, in caches, while the boar's winter store is internal – in its own body.

The richness of the autumn and early-winter food supply of acorns on the forest floor was extensively exploited by man in the Middle Ages. Stock of all sorts, not just pigs but also cattle, horses, sheep and goats, as well as geese, grazed beneath the oakwoods, creating a pressure which doubtless severely restricted the ability of the forests to regenerate, as almost all these animals would favour succulent young saplings. The swineherd would drive the pigs – usually a mixed herd, some belonging to the lord of the manor, others to villagers or to commoners – to the areas richest in fallen acorns, thereby exercising one of the ancient rights, that of the 'common of mast' or, as it is more often known, 'pannage'.

Towards the end of the winter, it is obvious that there are fewer thrushes about – even when the time of the evening roost arrives. This is partly because they have cleared up the berry crop and are now more widely distributed over the farmland, and partly because some mortality has occurred, but probably the major reason is that, having paused and fattened around the oak, many thrushes will have moved on. Sometimes this movement will be away to the west, the usual direction indicated by recoveries of ringed birds, but radar studies show that another possibility exists. Radar screens can be filmed using time-lapse photography to speed up the slow movements of echoes across the screen. Such films show bird movements very clearly – to such an extent that airport traffic controllers sometimes experience problems when attempting to sort planes from some larger birds or flocks of smaller ones. In eastern Britain, films show the early autumn bird arrivals from the east and north-east. From December to February there is an unexpected sight – echoes indicating many hundreds of thousands of birds, travelling south-eastwards into Europe, some of which may be the fieldfares and redwings from the oakwood, perhaps moving away from poor weather.

In a mild winter, a walk through the heronry down towards the bottom of the oakwood is always capable of producing a surprise. As in all dealings with the wild, this sort of visit must be accomplished infrequently and with stealth so that the colony is not disturbed. The first few days of bland weather will see a few birds roosting in the trees overnight, but by mid-February the unbelievably noisy honkings, screechings and bill-clappering of display may reach a crescendo. Astonishingly, the broad wings and long legs of the heron do not produce quite such an ungainly bird in the oaks as might be imagined. Steadying themselves with wings outstretched (like a tightrope walker with his pole), the herons pace sedately about on their spidery toes in the topmost twigs of the canopy, raising their crests and throwing back their heads in ecstasy on meeting their partner. This sexual arousal also brings a rosy flush to the normally yellow bill. The pair bond is sealed by copulation – again carried out in the treetops – and nesting proper starts.

Usually the majority of the nests in the heronry will have survived the winter's gales, and most birds, if they too have survived the hazards of the coldest season, will return to the nest they used the previous year. Naturally some changes of partner occur and new birds enter the breeding phase, but newcomers, whether from elsewhere or locally-bred youngsters nesting for the first time, will usually start much later in the season. For many years old-established pairs will occupy those nests which are both largest in bulk and, so far as can be judged, best-sheltered from the elements, especially cold winds. Always the first birds to be sitting tight, the activity of these old-stagers comes to be regarded as a sign that spring is on the way in earnest, although on several occasions they may be caught out and the female will later be seen sitting with a drift of snow on her back!

Nest building is often a repair job rather than a creative one, but there are complications as the presentation of sticks to the female is part of the ritual of courtship. Males, anxious to demonstrate their prowess, clamber around on high, seizing often quite sizeable branches (an inch or more in diameter) in their bills and attempting, sometimes with success, to snap them off. High in the trees such an operation can be tricky for a heavy bird and is rarely accomplished with any grace. The weaker brethren among the herons descend to the clearings and root around for dead branches, returning just as proudly as the others bearing gifts to their female. For many birds the temptations of a nearby untenanted or briefly unguarded nest are too strong to withstand and pilfering is rife.

The number of occupied nests grows as spring advances, with an accompanying increase in activity and in the cacophony. The most impressive sight of all is that of the females tucked down as low in the nest as possible riding out a March gale, all heads to wind. Some of the nests in more slender trees have been measured as moving through an arc of more than 15 feet (4·5 m) in a good gale – presumably a terrifying experience for those birds sitting. Once or twice in a decade birds will start to display, repair nests and even lay eggs at a startlingly early date, giving rise to the remarkable record of the first egg in January, and the last youngster leaving the colony at the beginning of October!

*Heronry*

So the days begin to lengthen; overall the temperatures are less harsh (though frosts and even snowfall always remain on the cards); green growth starts among the plants, including the oak, which from a distance takes on a misty, milky-yellow appearance rather than steely grey. Bird songs develop individually, and collectively conglomerate into the beginnings of a dawn chorus. Spring, for all its vicissitudes, has begun.

*Dormouse*

# Spring

HE first signs that spring has reached and warmed the roots of the oak are, strangely enough, best detected at a distance. Much as the willows in the low, damp part of the wood show signs of reawakening to a new season by turning that special primrose yellow about the twigs, so too does the oak very gradually shade from an inert brownish-grey towards pale green. For some reason, although the basis of this colour change is the gradual swelling of the bud, forcing open the brown bud-scales, it is more apparent standing back and viewing the tree as a whole than on close inspection.

The wonder of oncoming spring influenced primeval and medieval men strongly. Except in remote areas, it is left, in our modern and sometimes over-civilized society, to those with an interest in nature to appreciate such things. The mistle (or, in the past, missel) thrush enjoys a special popularity among country lovers as one of the earliest of songsters, and one of the most effective as a soloist. Warm days after the new year will see all the local males high in the treetops proclaiming territorial boundaries, and the mistle thrush that regularly uses some of the topmost twigs of our oak as song-posts is no exception. The bird's habit of continuing to sing in the teeth of the roughest of early spring gales has earned it the nickname 'storm cock'. The song is pure and simple, giving the impression that each note is carefully considered before production to make certain of best effect. It is melodious, and more akin to that of the blackbird than to the repetitious phrases of the song thrush.

Mistle thrushes nest very early – often in March. Almost every year a pair will choose the oak, their nest in the fork of a major branch a large, untidy construction built of grass and just about anything else that is handy: mistle thrushes were among the first birds to exploit waste polythene sheet as a nesting material, for example! Such nests are obviously very conspicuous, especially early in the season, and mistle thrushes rely on aggression to compensate for this. The bird's Welsh name, *penn-y-llwyn* – meaning 'master of the copse' – is an indication of this renowned quality. Magpies, jays and crows, although larger than the mistle thrush, are everyday targets, and even a buzzard will be treated to the thrush's wrath if it comes too near the nest. Marauding cats and foxes are vigorously and noisily dive-bombed, and mistle thrushes are usually among the first to raise the woodland alarm when a roosting owl is discovered. Although the attack is not often pressed home as far as physical contact, the fuss is usually sufficient to distract the intruder or drive it away.

As their name suggests, mistle thrushes are particularly partial to mistletoe berries. Aristotle was aware of this liking, and his name for them – *viscivorus* – is derived from the scientific name for the mistletoe (*Viscum*) and means 'mistletoe eater'. His epithet is retained in the scientific name for the mistle thrush itself, *Turdus viscivorus*. Although basically a woodland bird, it feeds much further out in open fields in summer than does the song thrush, and the young are especially conspicuous in their pale scaly plumage. In winter many other berries feature in its diet – even yew, where the poisonous pips pass through undigested. The mistle thrush is very fond of fallen apples too, not just those from the few crab-apple trees scattered through the wood, but also those that carpet the orchard floor in autumn, many so alcoholically over-ripe that intoxication could result!

Chaffinches, too, make an early start to the singing year: from February

*Mistle thrush*

onwards in the south, later in the north, their boisterous song – a long descending trill with a final characteristic swashbuckling flourish – can be heard from the oak. One of the marvels of bird song is how such complicated and often beautifully melodious phrases are passed on from one generation to the next. Are the songs learnt by each new generation, son listening to father and neighbouring males? Or does some genetic wizardry ensure that the egg hatches into a chick already 'programmed' with a song that will delight us next spring? Recent research at Cambridge University has gone some way to unravelling this mystery in the case of the chaffinch. It would seem from experiments that the basic framework of the song is inherited and will be produced automatically even by a young male chaffinch reared in total isolation from others of his kind. In the wild such a young male, possessing these instinctive foundations, will listen to his elders and gradually develop the quality, and the trills and flourishes, of his full song. In such a way, too, local dialects develop, making West Country chaffinches, for example, sound as distinctive as their human counterparts do to a visitor from, say, London.

The male chaffinch in spring is as unmistakable as his song, his plumage handsome with deep vinous pink breast, dove-grey head (with a black top-knot) and bold white wingbars on dark wings. In winter, he is rather drabber, more like the female, a mixture of beige and brown and well camouflaged in dead grass and stubble. How he changes from the one to the other is quite fascinating. At the end of the summer he replaces all his feathers in the annual moult. The body and head feathers that emerge as replacements all have broad buff or beige fringes, which give him his overall sombre appearance. As winter proceeds into spring, these fringes gradually wear off, revealing the beauty of his plumage beneath, and exposing it well in time for spring display. There is, too, a second benefit: the unworn feathers are produced in time for winter, when they offer the best protection as an insulating layer against the cold. As spring approaches and temperatures rise, such thick plumage is no longer necessary – indeed it may be on occasion an embarrassment, as birds, feather-clad, cannot sweat in the same way as mammals to lose heat. So the wear factor has a double advantage: a male chaffinch whose plumage is all but worn out at the start of spring is both at his most beautiful and well clad for the prevailing temperatures!

The female retains a camouflage-brown plumage throughout the year, the same subtle shades that hid her against the dead weeds and stubble protecting her from prying eyes as she sits, low in her nest, in the oak. Not just the female, but the nest also is well camouflaged. Usually it is set in a crotch close against the lichen-covered trunk, and is one of the neatest

*Chaffinch*

nests made by any bird. The basic cup is made of fine grasses and moss and lined with hair. The exterior is a marvel of concealment, for pieces of lichen are woven into the structure with cobwebs in a very lifelike, flaky fashion, so that it is difficult to be certain where tree ends and nest begins. This is important, as nesting starts early, often before leaves provide shelter.

In summer the chaffinches' diet is very varied and not as emphatically seed-biased as that of most finches. It includes small snails and worms, various fruits and seeds, and often aphids gathered high in the canopy of the oak. For the first few days of their lives, the birds feed their brood mostly on insect matter, and their beaks, relatively long-pointed (like tweezers) and slender for finches, are suitable both for this and the small-sized seeds that they tend to select. In winter, foraging is more often on the ground than in the treetops, and seeds then usually predominate in their diet.

A number of lichens clothe the bark of the oak, not only assisting the chaffinch in concealing its nest but adding a special beauty all their own, as they do in habitats as severe as the rocks just out of reach of the breaking waves on Britain's west coast, or as bizarre as modern corrugated asbestos farm buildings. Only in heavily industrialized areas do they fail to flourish, as they are particularly sensitive to levels of atmospheric sulphur dioxide. Because of this, an examination of the lichen flora can be a very sensitive indicator of environmental pollution.

Besides their intrinsic beauty, lichens are intriguing members of the plant kingdom, well worth a detailed look. Oak trees, it so happens, carry more varieties than any other tree species – perhaps thirty different lichens against twenty-three on the ash, next in the league table. The ragged bark provides an ideal footing for these 'hangers-on', or epiphytes as they are more properly called, where their root-like hyphae can collect moisture and supply the lichens' mineral requirements from sources like bird droppings and the other debris that accumulates in the bark fissures. Generally speaking, lichens and other epiphytic plants (including in Britain numerous mosses, liverworts and some ferns like the common polypody) flourish better in the damper conditions prevailing in oakwoods in the west and north, but our oak carries a good representative selection of the lichen types. Few of them have common names, but one exception is *Usnea ceratina*, a beard lichen (often wrongly called a beard moss), named after its bunches of wispy strands, which can withstand the conditions on the most exposed branches and twigs.

*Usnea ceratina*

Among the more conspicuous on the branches is *Ramalina farinacea*, velvety grey-green in colour and resembling bunches of minute upside-down reindeer antlers still clad in velvet. On some of the bigger branches running horizontally are a few plants of *Cetraria chlorophylla*, like miniature brown seaweeds amongst the moss. The yellowish, almost circular patches (reminiscent of those on the seaside rocks), best seen in spring before the oak leafs out and cuts down the light, are of *Parmelia caperata*, and several are saucer-sized as would be expected on a tree as big as our oak. At the base of the trunk is the rosette of another grey-green foliose lichen, with slender conical stalks, about $\frac{3}{4}$ inch (18 mm) high, standing erect, which help identify it as *Cladonia conicraea*.

Microscopic study, or even extended close examination through a hand

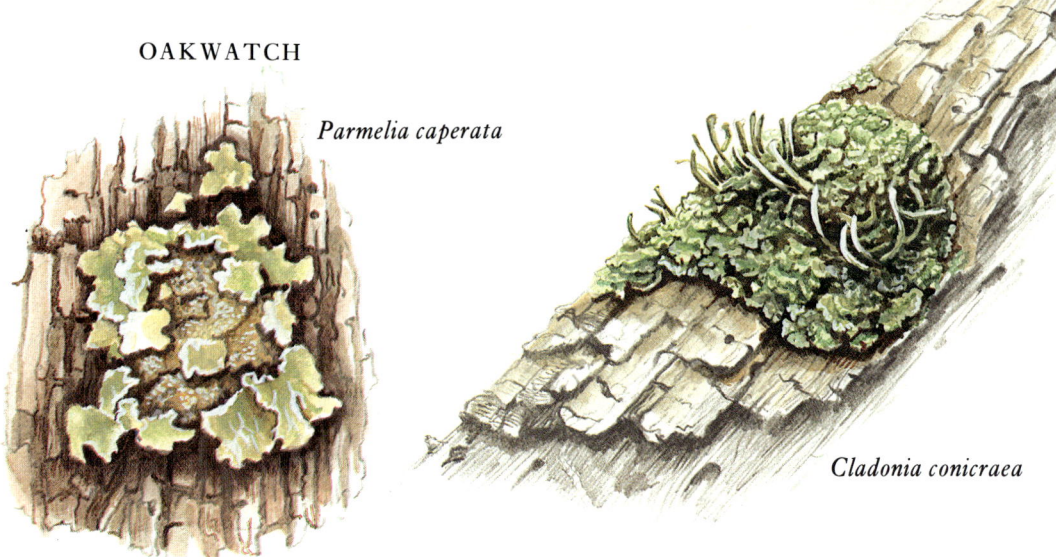

*Parmelia caperata*

*Cladonia conicraea*

lens, will show that each of these lichens has its own group of insects feeding on it. But what is more extraordinary is to look into the structure of the lichen itself. It would be all too easy to assume from their appearance – in many ways similar to the fungal moulds that take over the surface of neglected half-used jars of jam – that the lichens are just another fungus group, one that has made its home on tree bark, rocks and so on. Far from it: this lowly plant is in reality a highly organized co-operative, an inextricable mixture of fungus (which provides the matrix of hyphal filaments) and alga. The lichen forms when hyphae from the fungal 'partner' spread around and enclose cells of the alga. As the fungus grows, so more and more algal cells become involved, on the face of it taken over by a parasitic fungus. But the alga is far from the victim this seems to imply, as most cells carry on living and reproducing within the network of fungal hyphae. Clearly there are advantages to both sides here: the alga, with its green chlorophyll, does all the assimilation of carbon, thus providing the fungus with the organic food that it cannot manufacture for itself. In return, the alga is sheltered, and the root-like extremities of the fungus, locked into crevices in the bark, supply water and essential minerals for both partners, much more efficiently, it is thought, than the alga could on its own. Lichens are often long-lived, some perhaps enduring for decades, and certainly lasting vastly longer than the average life expectancy of an alga on its own. Technically this co-operative venture is one step up on symbiosis – which simply means 'living together' – and is called 'commensalism', to indicate that *both* partners derive benefit from their united living.

We often compare our birds unfavourably with their highly coloured cousins from tropical areas, but few tropical birds can compete with the vivid beauty of the green woodpecker. Often the first view is of a pigeon-

44

*Green woodpecker*

sized bird with deeply undulating flight, appearing to be made of pale gold as it swoops across the open ground in front of the oak. Following up for a closer view reveals its full beauty. It is difficult to believe that such greens and golds, set off by a scarlet cap and black, white and scarlet moustaches, could ever appear on a British bird!

One of the many old colloquial names for the green woodpecker is 'yaffle' – a word that well describes the ringing, laughing call, as much a feature of the bird as its gorgeous plumage. The green woodpecker is the largest of the British woodpeckers, and paradoxically spends much of its time on the ground rather than pecking wood. What it is doing is looking for ants. These insects, their eggs and larvae, and also on occasions various other insect grubs from rotten wood, are collected on the green woodpecker's tongue, one of the masterpieces of evolutionary adaptation. As in all woodpeckers it is surprisingly long: it can protrude for a couple of inches, and when not in active use lies coiled in a tubular sheath running beneath the lower jaw and up on to the top of the skull. This long tongue can be poked down ant runs, and is covered in a copious and very sticky layer of saliva, which traps the ants and obviously so gums them up as to immobilize them. So, when they are taken back to feed the hungry youngsters in their nest, nobody gets bitten or squirted with formic acid.

Woodpeckers excavate their own nest holes, sometimes in living softwood trees like conifers, but more commonly in dead or dying wood, especially in hardwood trees like oaks. Our oak has a major branch in this decaying condition, probably resulting from a lightning strike many years ago. Here the green woodpeckers have nested for several seasons. The hole is chiselled rather than hacked out, the beak being inserted into a crack and then twisted to prise off large flakes of wood. These chips are always a give-away for the nest site, as they show so fresh and white in spring against the sombre brown background of the previous year's fallen leaves. A short horizontal tunnel leads from the entrance hole to a vertical shaft several inches deep, ending in the flask-shaped nest chamber. Here a few wood chips serve as nest lining for the almost-spherical white eggs. Especially in their early days, the young are conspicuously ugly and reptilian, an appearance enhanced by their scanty covering of down. They are very fussily noisy, clearly a potential lure to predators as the young are deep in the hole and cannot themselves see danger coming. Hence the adult green woodpecker has a considerable repertoire of stern anxiety calls to warn them to be silent until the alarm is over.

Neither of the other two British woodpeckers actually nests in our oak, although both make regular use of it. The great spotted woodpecker – commonest and most widespread – is, like its green cousin, a conspicuous bird, with its pied plumage and scarlet patches. Its normal year-round call, a harsh and far-carrying 'tchack', or its staccato breeding-season 'drumming', quickly draw attention to its presence. Its deeply undulating method of flight, too, is conspicuous and characteristic, with a few flaps of the very rounded wings followed by a deep swooping glide, before the next series of flaps helps it to regain height.

Woodpeckers will always be seen perched head-up on tree trunks or branches. This is because, in the course of evolution, the tail feathers have become specially strengthened and inflexible, serving as a third leg, or prop, as the bird climbs and are used in much the same way as we would use a shooting-stick. This supplementary support aids a very powerful grip. Woodpecker legs are short but muscular, and the toes strong and tipped with long and very sharp claws to give an effective hold not just on the rugged oak but even on the smoothest-barked trees like beech. Unusually for birds, the toes are arranged two pointing forwards and two back to give optimum performance on a vertical surface. Thus woodpeckers move vertically or often in a spiral up the trunk, and occasionally laterally. When they have finished searching for food, they swoop off to the base of another tree or branch and begin to ascend once again. In the great spotted woodpecker the beak is relatively short, stout and sharp, with a squared-off end like a small chisel. This is an appropriate simile because the bird uses its beak as a combination of hammer and chisel, inserting the tip into the crack it has caused and using its powerful neck muscles to twist the beak and prise off flakes of wood.

One obvious question relating to woodpeckers is 'why do they not get splitting headaches?' The answer lies partly in the very robust bone structure of the skull, especially in front of the brain, and partly (in some or perhaps most woodpeckers) in the presence of a layer of shock-absorbing cartilaginous tissue, forming a cushion between the bones within the beak and the rest of the skull.

Adaptation does not stop here. The diet of the great spotted woodpecker is very varied, including a number of different types of seeds, fruit and nuts. Nuts are often brought to a well-used cleft in a favourite piece of bark on a big branch of the oak and hammered open while held in position in this natural vice. Another important food item is insects and their larvae. Often these may be found, perhaps sheltering during the winter, under easily-lifted flakes of bark, but the great spotted woodpecker is a specialist at extracting the wood-boring larvae that actually tunnel into the tree. Perched on the trunk, the bird can sense the approximate location of the grub, perhaps hearing minute sounds of movement or chewing as it gnaws away. A few swift pecks and an opening is hacked into the tunnel, and then the woodpecker's enormously long tongue comes into play. It can be extended for a couple of inches up the tunnel, and it has a sharp, barbed, horny tip which harpoons the luckless grub and drags it out to be eaten.

The natural all-the-year-round diet is augmented at various times with rather surprising items. The great spotted woodpecker has a marked taste for the nestlings of other birds, and is adept at catching them. As they grow, the nestlings of most hole-nesting birds like the tits jump up to the nest hole as the parent birds approach, alerted by the shadow of the adult falling across the hole. The woodpecker has capitalized on this, and as *its* shadow falls across the hole and a young tit jumps up in order to be the first to be fed, the woodpecker reaches in and grabs it, dragging it out to hack up and eat on a more usual perch. Sometimes woodpeckers learn to associate this food supply with nestboxes put up for tits and will chisel their way in through the back to get at eggs or young!

When the male great spotted woodpecker wants to advertise for a mate and later mark the boundary of his territory, he 'drums' on an appropriately resonant dead piece of branch near the top of our oak. On occasion woodpeckers will seek special effects by drumming on a corrugated iron roof! For many years controversy raged over just *how* the noise was produced. Many skilled ornithologists argued that they could *see* that it was made vocally, much as we can 'roll rs' with our tongue curled. Only in the 1930s was the issue settled by embedding microphones in regularly used drumming branches to show that it *was* a rapid succession of physical taps by the beak that caused the noise. Even after this the acrimonious argument between experts rumbled on for several years!

Compared with the short and powerful bursts of drumming by the great spotted, the lesser spotted woodpecker drums at a noticeably higher pitch and in 'drum-rolls' of about twice as long duration. This would perhaps be expected of a bird which compares in size with its great spotted cousin as a sparrow would with a thrush. The lesser spotted woodpecker is by no means as common a visitor to the oak – perhaps because there are only a couple of suitably slender resonant branches, but more likely because nowhere is it a very numerous bird. Old county bird reports and the bird books of Victorian times and earlier indicate that this was not always the case, and that in the latter half of the last century the lesser spotted was the commoner woodpecker and the great spotted the rarer. It would be fascinating to know the reasons for the change: perhaps they are in some way connected with the underlying causes of the current growth in numbers of the lesser spotted woodpeckers. For some reason these birds seem to have profited particularly from the food supply and nest-site availability resulting from the Dutch elm disease outbreak of the last decade. It is pleasing that

*Yellow archangel*

*Dog's mercury*

*Bluebell*

at least some small benefit has come from a disease that has otherwise so drastically altered and scarred our landscape.

Spring is the time that botanically the surroundings of the oak are at their most picturesque. In the main clearings the gorse is well and truly ablaze with colour and strikingly bright against the leafless darkness of the surrounding trees. The blackthorn, despite the inroads that the bullfinches have made into its flower buds during the winter, has turned from sombre leaden patches to drifts of unbelievably solid white blossom. Simple, common plants these, functional as far as wildlife is concerned winter through, providing food and, perhaps almost more important, shelter from the elements at their worst. Now they are both emotionally and aesthetically satisfying, typical of spring.

Much the same can be said of the plants beneath the oak itself. Most of these must seize the opportunity to grow and flower with some urgency in the early weeks of spring: if they are held back too long, the oak will be leafing out and in a matter of days much of the light filtering through the bare branches to the woodland floor will be excluded by a green curtain. For the small plants beneath the oak, this light is vital to the process of

49

photosynthesis: each leaf is a minute green biochemical factory wherein water and atmospheric gases are converted into carbohydrates – the sugars and starches of plant food – in the catalytic presence of the leaf's chloroplasts and powered by the sun's energy.

*Moschatel*

Thus many of the typical oak woodland spring plants appear suddenly, to human eyes, and are over all too soon. Some, like the tiny, green-flowered moschatel, often called 'clocktower plant' because of the four-square way its florets are arranged, just like a microscopic Big Ben, are inconspicuous in the extreme. Moschatel and the equally diminutive golden saxifrage are good indicators of damp patches of soil: they are moisture-lovers, growing best on heavy damp clays close to springs. The flowers on dog's mercury are almost as unnotice-able, but the plant itself is often 8 inches (20 cm) or more high. Interesting comparisons

*Golden saxifrage*

can be obtained between dog's mercury growing in the open and that tucked away under the deepest cover. Using a photographic light meter to record the available light, and a ruler to measure the height of plants in the cluster, it becomes clear that dog's mercury is a good survivor of poor light conditions – where often (say, underneath dense hawthorn scrub) it is the only plant to grow. Nevertheless the plants beneath the oak, better lit, are both bigger and lusher. Moving out into the full sunlight of the clearing, it is at once apparent that the plants are smaller again, with darker, more leathery leaves, and are having trouble surviving against the competition of grasses, brambles and bracken that flourish so much better in open light: a clear case of each to his own.

March is perhaps the best month to see the impact of aspect on plant life: the importance of which way the plants are facing. Dawdling on the south-west-facing slopes in the wood, each year it comes as a surprise to discover just how much more advanced the plants are here than elsewhere, with a combination of protection from the north-easters and the additional warmth from the sun. Bud burst may be up to a fortnight earlier, and under the thin canopy of the oak trees the scattering of violets shows to best effect.

Fringing the paths and grassy areas are the bolder splashes of colour from some very robust primroses, benefiting from the rich soil and deep leaf litter.

Beneath our oak, however, it is the wood sorrel and wood anemone that are the first to show. The wood sorrel or oxalis, with delicate nodding flowers on stalks a few centimetres high, is the confusing one. The leaves, which appear earlier than the flowers (each five-petalled, a fine white with a pale pink tracery of veins), are composed of three leaflets, are heart-shaped and look very like a clover, although they are often held folded, like a tent. Clovers, however, are in the pea family, lovers of the open land in general and in no way related to the *Oxalis* family. As is the case with a number of other wild flowers, wood sorrel blossoms are sensitive to light, and old country lore would have it that you can tell the time of day by the degree to which the flowers have opened out into bells. This may be almost as tricky as telling the time by a sundial on a day when clouds and bright spells are alternating, but does provide an area of fascination and intrigue for those with time, and again a small ruler, a light meter and the inclination to investigate the problem. Does, for example, a thin, high-overcast sky, often painfully bright to human eyes, have the same effect on the plant as bright sunlight?

The wood anemone, a member (despite appearances) of the buttercup family, must be one of the best-loved spring sights as a carpet beneath our oak and countless others across Britain. The lacy, fern-like, grey-green fronds of the leaves appear first, quickly followed by nodding, multi-petalled flowers that move, as the plant's alternative name of 'windflower' suggests, with the slightest of breezes. The white flowers with their yellow core are made the more attractive by a pale purple blush to the undersides of the petals.

Anemones are more numerous where the wind has reduced the accumulation of leaf litter to a minimum: on the sheltered side of the oak, and stretching away into the surrounding woodland, the litter of leaves may be several centimetres deep. In a mild winter the leaves of the bluebells will have been visible for some weeks, pushing up hyacinth-like, rich glossy green against the flat brown. As spring progresses, they too burgeon into their full glory. It could easily be argued that sheets of bluebells, as a spectacle, are so familiar as to be perhaps too 'chocolate boxy', but that argument would never be advanced by anyone who each year enjoyed the experience of seeing – and, almost as important, smelling – the bluebell blaze. Beneath our oak in most years the showing is good, but deeper into the wood, where a number of aged trees have fallen and rotted away to leave a large clearing, sheltered by surrounding trees and criss-crossed only by

fox, badger and rabbit pathways, the beauty may take your breath away.
In the open this spectacle is soon masked by the appearance of the first
brownish swan-necks of the oncoming summer's bracken, but beneath the
oak the light is too poor for this plant and the bluebells fade and set their
lumpy seed pods, which remain visible through the year as they brown and
dry, finally releasing numerous small black seeds.

Coming into bloom just after the bluebells reach their prime, yellow
archangel adds to the colour spectrum. This relative of the dead-nettles,
with its hooded, pulpit-like red-veined yellow flowers in clusters round the
stem, each cluster supported by a pair of saw-edged leaves, can apparently
endure the fading light as the oak leaves expand, and will flower on into
the summer. Another shade specialist, again capable of flowering into the
summer, and indeed under the oak not normally *starting* to bloom until June
or July, is enchanter's nightshade. Most of the willowherbs, to which the
shorter enchanter's nightshade is closely related, are quite large plants with
wind-dispersed seeds. A good example is the fireweed or rose-bay
willowherb, spectacularly pink and common on all sorts of waste ground,
including those areas of rubble remaining after parts of our cities had been
destroyed in the blitz. The fluffy white seeds of rose-bay are blown great
distances on the wind like thistledown, and on a windy day the 'snowstorm'
of seed dispersal is almost as spectacular as the blossom. Unlike its relatives,
enchanter's nightshade has round instead of elongated seed pods, and a
close-up look through a hand lens shows each bulbous structure to be
covered in dozens of small hooks. These barbs indicate a totally different
means of seed dispersal as they would latch, Velcro-like, on to the fur of
any passing animal such as a squirrel scurrying around in search of early-
fallen acorns. Such a technique is better suited to the normally relatively
sheltered ground beneath the oak than the wind dispersal more common
among the willowherbs.

But what of the oak itself? Those hard round brown buds have burst
open still further, and together with the emerging and gradually unfolding
yellow-green leaves come the flowers. These are of two sorts. The male
flowers are catkin-like tassels almost reminiscent of Victorian bell pulls, with
several clusters of tiny florets at intervals down a stalk a few inches long.
The female flowers, and it is these that will ultimately form the acorns when
fertilized, are much less obvious. Looking like tiny part-opened buds, but
showing no leaves, all that protrudes to collect the wind-blown pollen –
there being plenty of wind in the canopy – are three tiny reddish styles.

In a year of good blossom, the oak will be covered in the golden tassels
of the male flowers. It and its neighbours will be slightly out of phase with
one another, just as they often will be in autumn when the leaves are shed.

For birds like the woodpigeon and the bullfinch, eager for a change of diet after the relatively dry bud and seed foods of winter, this extension to the period of availability of oak flowers as food must be most welcome. For all or most of the year, bullfinches eat a variety of wild natural foods. In spring oak flowers come first, and then they concentrate on the seeds of dandelion, buttercup and many other plants as summer progresses, turning to nettle and later dock in the autumn. As winter closes in, most seeds fall, but dock and bramble remain available. After Christmas, these seeds are supplemented by ash keys until, late in winter, the buds of blackthorn and hawthorn elsewhere in the wood begin to swell to a worthwhile size. Many bullfinches will survive perfectly well all their lives on this natural diet, and it seems that only when natural supplies fail for some reason do those birds resident close to gardens or orchards turn their attention to cultivated varieties. When they do, they may find them such a palatable alternative that the forthcoming summer's fruit crop is almost destroyed.

Without doubt, the bullfinch *is* a beautiful bird, the male scarlet-breasted, grey-backed and black-capped, this cardinal-like garb giving rise to the colloquial German name '*Dompfaff*' ('cathedral priest'). The female is a subtle mixture of suede-browns, but still with the black cap. Both possess a purplish-black tail and strikingly white patch on the rump, so often all that we see as they dart away deep into the bushes. But let no one doubt the other side of the bullfinch character. Beneath that black cap is a sharp, slightly hooked beak, rather rounder in profile than the typical wedge-shaped beak of a finch and ideal for nipping off whole buds from trees and shrubs and biting out the core. This process is so lightning-fast that gooseberry buds can be husked and devoured at the staggering rate of thirty per minute!

Since the time of Queen Elizabeth, the bullfinch has had a price on its head. Even in those far-off, poorly-documented days, gardeners and fruit growers were sufficiently incensed by the havoc caused by bullfinches eating flower buds during the winter (most attacks occur in January and February) for the chroniclers of the time to note that one penny reward was on offer for 'everie Bulfynche or other Byrde that devoureth the blowthe of fruit'. Many gardeners or fruit growers of the present day, surveying the wreckage after bullfinches have been feeding (the scattered litter is painfully conspicuous on top of the snow), see so many bud fragments that they assume that nothing could have been eaten and that the devastation was sheer wanton vandalism. Not a bit of it: the attack is not only technically skilful, but purposeful. Deep in the heart of the bud lies the flower initial – in a pear bud about the size of a pin-head and looking like a miniature cauliflower. Here, not surprisingly, much of the 'goodness' (in nutritional

*Male bullfinch and oak blossom*

terms) of the bud is concentrated,
and it is this that the bullfinches are
sensibly seeking when they discard the
residue of the bud to feed as effectively as
possible. To the annoyance of the gardener,
they always seem to make a more destructive
job than when devouring the buds of the wild oak.

Although dependent on the oak for just this relatively short but
nonetheless critical time early in spring, the bullfinch is among the most
sedentary of birds, and rarely will those eating the oak's male flowers stray
far away. They will breed elsewhere in the wood, deep in the prickly shelter
of hawthorn, blackthorn, gorse or bramble, and during the breeding season
the male is rarely far from his female's side, often singing his whispering,
wheezy song. This sounds like a gently swinging, creaking gate, very
different from the more familiar, clearly penetrating whistle that the birds
use to keep in contact with one another in dense undergrowth or while
feeding together up in the oak's canopy. They will collect food together,
often far from the nest, carrying it back in hamster-like cheek pouches to

feed the brood on the flat, fragile and twiggy nest, built just like a miniature woodpigeon's.

Another group of mobile creatures which, while not in the strictest sense dependent solely on the oak, must find the tree's long-term presence in the wood of utmost value, are the bats. That same lightning-struck massive dead branch that holds the green woodpecker's nest from time to time also has a hollow interior, reached through a jagged hole. Within this hollow, bats hibernate during the winter and shelter during the summer months. The vast majority of them, and sometimes the gathering may exceed one hundred individuals, are pipistrelles, our smallest variety of bat.

With a wingspan of about 8 inches (20 cm) and a weight of between 5 and 10 grams, pipistrelles are the most widely distributed as well as the most numerous of British bats. They feed mostly on small insects like gnats, though occasionally attacking larger prey like moths. They secrete themselves in the slenderest of cracks within the hollow and, despite their pungent smell, take some seeking out with a torch. Although quiescent in hibernation from late October until, usually, early March, their hibernation is not a deep one, and on the occasional mild evenings of winter – the sort that seemingly out of nowhere conjure up an amazing and unseasonal dancing cloud of midges – they can be seen flying about, often high up. As a rule of thumb, it is the appearance in spring of those first columns of gnats and midges that signal the regular appearance of the pipistrelles from their roosting place, for this it has now become.

*Pipistrelle*

After a few weeks of good feeding, the females ovulate, usually during May, and the egg is fertilized. But here the story departs markedly from the pattern of mammalian birth so familiar to us and differing only in time scale from animal to animal, including man. In many, if not most, British bats the actual mating takes place some time during the autumn. There seem to be no fixed pair bonds, and copulation appears to be promiscuous within the confines of the colony – the hollow branch in our oak. Once mating has occurred, the female stores the male's sperm in her oviduct through the winter hibernation, and the spring, until she releases her egg for fertilization. In the pipistrelle, there is usually a single youngster, born blind, naked and helpless after a gestation period of about six weeks – a long time for so small a creature. In the first few days after the birth, the female pipistrelles clamber awkwardly out of the branch with their youngster clinging to them, but soon its weight and encumbrance proves too much and the growing infant is left, tucked away in a crack in the roost, for about three weeks before it becomes independent. During this period it suckles from its mother when she returns to the roost.

Occasionally, or perhaps quite commonly, as relevant observations carried out regularly and in detail are rare, the pipistrelle mob is joined in the dead branch by individuals of a larger species, the noctule. Weighing from 20 to 40 grams and with a wingspan about double that of the pipistrelle at 16 inches (40 cm), the noctule with its chunky build, high flight (much better sustained and less flickering than the smaller bats), and its habit of indulging in frequent dives, is quickly distinguished from its cousin. During the summer, noctules often change their roosting quarters, so it may be that the oak sees quite a number of individuals during the season, even if only one is visible at a time as it hunts beetles and moths. Noctules leave the roost early to hunt, often well before sunset, flying noisily with a metallic squeaking call for an hour or more after dusk and for a similar period just before dawn.

Most of the noises made by bats are at the limit of human hearing or beyond. The calls of the noctule are an exception, for they are usually easily heard, but their purpose is the same as the ultrasonic notes of others. Experiments to discover how bats, with their feeble eyesight, manage to avoid obstacles in flight and catch their prey, often fast-moving insects, in mid-air, began as long ago as the end of the eighteenth century in Italy. Initially it was thought that some sense of touch was responsible, associated with the peculiar leaf-like protruberances that many bats have on their faces, but by 1920 pioneer research work indicated that these mammals emit ultrasonic pulses which are reflected from nearby objects and give them information about their position and nature – whether they are obstacles or food! It has now been shown that many bats do emit these high-frequency squeaks, and the theory of 'echo-location', where the bat uses its unusually elaborate ears to decode the reflected echoes, is now generally accepted. It has even been discovered that some potential prey – various insects – have evolved counter-echo-location mechanisms, themselves producing noises that effectively confuse or jam the 'enemy radar', allowing the intended victim to escape.

Watching our oak through the year, it never ceases to amaze that behind the wealth of fascination that it offers lies a range of biological adaptation, by both plants and animals, that closely parallel what we commonly term the 'marvels of modern science'. Good examples are the Velcro-like seeds of the enchanter's nightshade and the 'sonar' of the bats, but in one field, as yet imperfectly understood by man, nature has far outstripped the best that man can do in terms of endurance, accuracy of timing and perfection of navigation, and miniaturization. She has done so in migration.

By spring most of the migrant thrushes that characterized the winter, the fieldfares and redwings, will have moved off eastward and no longer do huge starling flocks commute to and from the roost in the wood. March, at its close, is to some extent a month in limbo, for the bulk of winter birds have gone, and most of the summer birds have yet to come. The herald of the summer birds may be here, though, and on every warm March day ears should be kept cocked for the one summer song (besides that of the cuckoo) that needs no re-learning each year. In time, sure enough, a chiff-chaff will lisp away on a topmost twig of the oak – and memory may often serve correctly if it suggests that last year's first chiff-chaff sang from the same twig.

As the spring develops, so more and more migrants appear. For the earlier ones, it is almost possible to predict the sort of day (or rather night, for most birds are night migrants, resting and feeding by day) on which arrivals will occur. Ideal are calm, clear nights with a little wind, or with light airs with a touch of north or east in them. Little movement will take place in heavy cloud, or in blustery wet weather. Sometimes April will catch a hangover from March by way of a few squally days and nights at a stretch, and somewhere to the south of the track of the cyclonic weather (or depression) across the Atlantic, the hordes of migrants will be held up. While the dam holds, the wood is quiet – there will be some song from the thrushes, blackbirds and other residents, but even the early-arrival chiff-chaffs have fallen silent, perhaps because they need in these unfavourable times to spend much of their day feeding sufficiently hard and fast to maintain life. Ultimately, the dam must break – and the metaphor is not misplaced, for at the first sign of a suitable spell of weather, the interrupted migrants press on northwards even more anxiously.

Such an occurrence is an almost annual 'event' at the network of bird observatories around Britain's coast – especially those along the southern approaches. Sometimes the bushes, and even the grass, on the islands or promontories where the observatories are situated seem to be a moving carpet of newly arrived but tired and hungry birds, seeking to feed up as quickly as possible so that further progress is not impeded. The term 'fall' that is applied to such an arrival is not at all inappropriate. In the wood things are a little different: after a few stormy, sullen days, a calm, mild and fine morning arrives, and everywhere, including in the canopy of the oak, there are willow warblers singing! The other species that tend to arrive conspicuously like this are the turtle dove and the whitethroat and lesser whitethroat, but although their advance guard often arrives in the wood in April, the bulk of these three species will not usually reach us until early May.

Other less conspicuously dramatic arrivals during April are the blackcaps, followed after two or three weeks by the garden warblers. In the early days, both species spend a lot of time foraging in the oak, but soon the garden warbler moves away into shrubbier areas, leaving the blackcap, which prefers tall trees, to sing solo from its canopy. For some reason, the first cuckoo to call from the oak never achieves a calibre of earliness meriting a mention in the correspondence of *The Times*.

While the mistle thrushes in the oak are now feeding young, and blackbirds and song thrushes are well away elsewhere in the wood on the first of what, for some pairs at any rate, may be four or five broods if the season remains favourable right through, the remainder of the residents are at least building nests. Some of these other species appear as if from nowhere to become strikingly apparent. They may have been about winter through, but are then much less significant for some reason: the best examples are linnets, chaffinches and yellowhammers. Perhaps the difference is that they roost, relatively quietly and certainly inconspicuously, in large numbers of which only a few pairs remain in the wood to breed. Certainly the males of each are noticeable enough in April – the chaffinch largely by its superb song from within the oak's canopy, the other two species more because of the prominent bush-top song-posts that they occupy in the woodland clearings. While the linnet has a pleasant song, if just a little jingly and unformed, surely only a female yellowhammer could find the dry, rasping notes of the male at all attractive. (These bear little, if any, resemblance to the reputed 'a-little-bit-of-bread-and-no-cheese'.)

But to return to the first chiff-chaff. Bird ringing is a scientific study in which individually marked, lightweight metal bands (following the same principle as a car registration number plate) are placed round the legs of birds. On the band, or ring, is a return address so that birds found dead can be reported, and of course the bird ringers themselves can re-catch the bird in a net or trap to follow its progress. The disturbance to the individual bird is minimal, and the ring causes no harm or annoyance, but the information gathered into the data bank operated by the British Trust for Ornithology is of immense value. Initially, in the early days of the ringing

scheme at the start of this century, the most exciting reports concerned the
destinations overseas of our summer visitors after their return migration,
but today more importance is attached to supplementary evidence on
aspects like the routes migrants take and the hazards associated with them;
changes in weight and plumage through the various seasons; causes of
death; life-spans; and to detailed studies of the birds in a particular area
– like the woodland around our oak – based on a series of recapture records
through the year. Thus it is that we can say, based on an ever-growing
dossier of information, that many adult migrants (not the young birds) may
return to much the same territory in consecutive years. Such is the case
for the chiff-chaff singing in the oak: this tree was the major song-post in
its territory last year, and will be again in this. Since last seen and heard,

*Chiff-chaff*

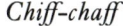

this very fragile and rather drab 7 grams of bird has probably wintered by the Mediterranean or perhaps even further south. And in a head smaller than the size of your little finger's last joint is the control centre not only of the everyday functions of the bird, but also of navigation equipment capable of getting it back to its territory with precision!

All through the summer this aspect of bird migration will be rediscovered: not only can the young cuckoo reach Africa unaided by its parents (except that in the genetic sense they have contributed to its instinctive abilities), but the whole business involves meticulous accuracy. From the marked birds recaptured each year after they have spent the winter in Africa may be built up a picture on a national scale. Adult birds – that is, those that are breeding – if they survive the rigours of the migration journeys (even this seems close to a miracle!) are most likely to return not just to the same county, but to the same wood, and to the same area in that wood, no matter how small. Similarly, allowing for the inevitable regularity of deaths and for occasional 'divorces', the swallows in the porch or garage of a house are likely to be the self-same birds from one year to the next.

The young birds reared in the wood, however, seem to distribute themselves more widely. Because the mortality amongst the young is so much higher, and because (obviously) it is easier to study a bird that returns precisely to an area where bird ringers are working regularly, it is more difficult to draw sound conclusions on the evidence available. Nevertheless, a generally wider distribution of returning young birds about to embark on their first breeding season would seem evolutionarily sound, for in this way the dangers of inbreeding (pooh-poohed, perhaps with justice, by some biologists today) are avoided, and any local deficiencies such as a breeding failure for one reason or another are remedied rather than being followed by a local extinction of that particular species.

Given the metronomic repetitiousness of its song, the chiff-chaff is hardly likely to register as a member of the warbler family to anybody other than the ornithologically well-informed. Most males, especially in the excitement of early spring, setting up territories and attracting mates, manage to stumble even over their own names, producing 'chiff-chiff-chaffs' and 'chaff-chaff-chiffs' as often as not, and hardly qualify even as songbirds. The willow warbler is quite different. If ever a songbird deserved to be called 'harbinger of spring' it is this one. The silvery descending trill of song immediately conjures up visions of yellow-green early oak leaves just bursting from the bud, dappled spring sunshine on primrose banks and perhaps, too, the sweetness of the smell of woodland carpeted in bluebells.

Unlike the chiff-chaff – a near relative almost impossible to distinguish save by its vastly different, monotonous 'chiff-chaff' song – the willow warbler migrates far south to the tropics of Africa for the winter. Most birds moult – to replace worn-out feathers – once a year, but not the willow warbler. This tiny scrap of birdlife, weighing 10 grams, moults twice, once before it goes and once again in Africa just before it returns. That something so small can successfully endure the enormous double journey beyond the equator and back, *and* find the energy to replace its plumage twice each year, should fill us with amazement. Add to it the pin-point navigational accuracy (as in the chiff-chaff) that the adults achieve in returning to precisely the same patch of woodland in successive years and you wonder whether mankind is right to glory in his inventions of navigational computers or even (considering the tiny size of a willow warbler brain) in the microchip!

While the chiff-chaff pair nest almost every year in the rough grass, bracken and bramble only a few feet from the base of the oak, the willow warbler is not a regular resident because it prefers scrubby areas like blackthorn and hawthorn thickets to the dense woodland of tall trees. In consequence, it has a much wider habitat adaptability than the chiff-chaff that enables it to penetrate silver-birch scrub right up to the extreme north of Scotland, while the chiff-chaff becomes thin on the ground after the Borders. Even open moorland areas are being made more acceptable to willow warblers by re-afforestation schemes, the young conifer plantations being ideal habitat. The willow warbler seems now to be establishing itself as our most numerous and widespread summer migrant, considerably commoner than the swallow.

When the willow warbler does nest close to the oak, the nest is usually very well concealed, more or less on the ground in thick long grass and with a dome of woven grass stems overhead, unlike that of the chiff-chaff which is usually a foot and sometimes a yard or more above ground level. In high summer, the adult willow warbler feeds a lot on small insects, often catching them on the wing or plucking aphids from the leaves of the oak, hovering almost like a hummingbird while it does so. At this time, it occasionally comes into conflict with its relatives and tempers flare visibly. Usually it is the larger willow warbler that wins the show of strength (actual fights are rare), even though the chiff-chaff is more properly the bird for this particular niche in the woodland habitat. In no way are willow warblers averse to tackling larger prey when an opportunity arises, and they can sometimes be seen on a grassy track struggling to subdue a large green caterpillar seemingly as big as themselves. Always appearing busily industrious, willow warblers normally manage to raise two broods each summer, sometimes three. Attractively, they also manage to find time to sing between broods, keeping the summer woodland full of superb sound.

Certainly the cuckoo should not be regarded as a harbinger of spring, as it is such a late migrant. An anonymous thirteenth-century poet had it right when he wrote:

> Sumer is icumen in, lhude sing cuccu!

But the cuckoo is an amazing bird, its life-cycle an essay in the marvels of evolution. In Britain, most cuckoos are associated with one of three common foster parents: the reed warbler in marshland, the meadow pipit on

*Baby cuckoo and dunnock*

moorland, and the dunnock on farmland and in woodland. Thus it is the plentiful population in the wood of dunnocks (which used to be called hedge sparrows despite their obviously fine-pointed insect-eating beak) that the cuckoo seeks from the branches of the oak.

Consider for a moment, however, the eggs of these three common foster parents: those of the reed warbler are greenish-white with grey and brown freckles; those of the meadow pipit have brown and grey spots and squiggles so dense that the paler ground colour is almost obliterated; and the dunnock's eggs are strikingly sky-blue and lacking any markings. These are considerable differences in both colouration and habitat, but even a cuckoo laying for the first time will be able to seek out the correct habitat and host, so that her eggs will be close enough imitations to fool the foster parents. She will hunt through her territory, often spying from the oak's branches to locate foster dunnock nests and laying as soon as they are ready with a part-complete or recently completed clutch.

Egg laying takes only a moment in a swift visit. The cuckoo's wings hardly stop beating as she lands on the nest, lays her egg, snatches up a dunnock egg and departs. The cuckoo egg is specially quick to develop, taking only ten or eleven days, and is usually a couple of days faster than those of the host. The chick that emerges is a muscular baby and, wriggling beneath its unfortunate foster brothers and sisters (or any remaining eggs), arches its back, braces itself with its embryo wings – and hoists them up and out over the side of the nest, where of course they perish.

Thereafter, the baby cuckoo grows at a furious pace, soon dwarfing the nest and its foster parents, who must be driven mad by its incessant, but obviously very effective, wheedling cries for food. Even after it has left the

nest – by which time the adult cuckoos have all departed for Africa – the fledgling produces a call that will stop *any* food-carrying parent in its tracks and draw it, like a powerful magnet, to stuff its beakful into the tempting orange gape of the young cuckoo. At least one unfortunate wren is on record as having overdone things by falling into that capacious throat, suffocating both the cuckoo and itself!

Then comes the last episode of this amazing story. A month or more after the adults have migrated, the young cuckoos set off on their own, with nothing save their instinctive navigation systems to guide them, for the wintering areas in tropical Africa.

Towards the end of spring, and as much as anything to emphasize the differences between residents and migrants, it is worth the walk down to the lower end of the oakwood to see the heronry established in the big oaks there. Most heronries have been in existence for many years, some for centuries, like that in Chilham in Kent, which is noted in Kirkby's *Inquest*, a manuscript published in about 1290 in the reign of Edward I. It is fascinating to see that today, almost 700 years later, it differs little in size and location. The oakwood heronry has a similar but not quite so long history, and has moved about the wood to some degree. Established long ago in oaks close to our tree, it moved by degrees into some tall elms that formed the fringing hedgerow to the bottom of the wood. Perhaps eighty years ago these ceased to be trimmed, and soon became the tallest trees around, naturally enticing the herons which in general favour being as on top of the world as they can be, for safety's sake. All went well, and the heronry expanded for some years, until with the swift onset of Dutch elm disease more than a decade ago, the elms began dying back rapidly. True to the old adage that dead or dying trees are soon vacated, the herons moved steadily back into the nearby oaks as the elms toppled or were felled.

Following an open winter, even in late March a quiet walk beneath the nests might reveal the 'tick-tick-tick' of newly hatched heron chicks. Certainly this is the heronry sound of April, and as the chicks grow their voices deepen to a 'tock-tock-tock' – produced with metronomic regularity when they are hungry. They always seem to be in this state – and as there may be as many as four or five nestlings in each family, their parents have their work cut out keeping them fed, especially in a large colony like this where they may have to fly a few miles to find a free stretch of water for fishing. To feed their young, the parent birds regurgitate a crop of eels, fish and frogs, plus the occasional water vole or snake – often not quite dead – into the bottom of the nest, adding a further guttural dimension to the extraordinary cacophony that is part of everyday life in a heronry.

Searching under the nests from which noises emanate will give us a chance of finding the hatched eggshells and assessing now many chicks have appeared. Heron eggs are only a little bigger, if anything, than those of a chicken, and are bright pale blue. Those that have successfully hatched can be identified by the even chipping round the largest 'equator', and by the presence of a transparent and now drying membrane, containing many brownish blood vessels, on the inside of the shell. Those that have not been so successful and owe their hatched appearance to the attack of a predator – usually a member of the crow family – can be just as quickly identified, as they are not broken equatorially but usually show signs of a jagged-edged 'stab' wound from a substantial beak. Save for a few traces of dried yolk, the inside is clean and white, and often dried yolk adheres to the outside of the shell. This technique for separating those eggs lost to predators from those that have hatched successfully applies to pretty well all birds.

But the heronry contains not just herons. Beside it – and the margins of the two intermingle – is a rookery, whose inhabitants were presumably seeking a colony site as safe as that of the herons and were doubtless stimulated to some degree by the presence of the larger birds, although aerial battles are so commonplace in spring that it is evident that neighbourly relations are not too easy at best. Any fine day from midwinter onwards, but preferably one with a fresh breeze, rooks will be seen over or near their rookery, throwing themselves about in the sky in an aerobatic spectacular. Although much of this aerial cavorting may be linked with display and pair formation for the coming breeding season, or with learning and developing vital flying skills, with rooks (and other members of the crow family) it is difficult to be certain that there is not some element of sheer enjoyment involved, so recklessly enthusiastic do they seem and so pointless otherwise their manoeuvres.

*Crow*

*Rook*

An old adage would suggest that rooks and the slightly larger but otherwise similar carrion crow can be separated on the basis that one on its own will be a crow while a flock together will be rooks. This is only broadly true, and a closer inspection is needed to be certain. The carrion crow is dark all over, matching its evil reputation, while the feathers of the rook have a superb purple iridescence when seen well. Crows have a dark beak and a pronounced 'Roman nose', while rooks have a straight-edged, pale, dagger-like beak, ending (in the adults) in conspicuous pale cheek patches. These are whitish, featherless skin, and expand (like a hamster's cheek pouches) to carry food back to the young in the nest. A final distinguishing feature is that rooks have a 'baggy-trousered' appearance to their leg feathers, while carrion crows seem to be wearing tight-fitting stockings on the upper part of their legs. A pair of carrion crows used to nest in the oak itself until a grey squirrel took over their untidy, bulky structure as a drey one winter, and the crows have not returned since.

The rookery itself is a township in the sky, with its own complex community structure and, like modern human communities, its social problems. The older birds nest in safer, centrally situated sites, in large nests created over several years. Newcomers are relegated to the fringes of the colony. The birds are aggressively possessive of their site, and of their nest material, but the minute a back is turned, petty thieving of twigs occurs, ensuring that the rookery is in perpetual turmoil and a cacophony of noise: all very similar to the heronry alongside.

That is not all. A closer look at the herons' nests shows that some – the older and bulkier structures – have other tenants. In the very biggest, a few pairs of jackdaws find cavities large enough to nest in. These grey-capped smaller relatives of the rook are perhaps the most likely culprits when it comes to attacking unguarded herons' eggs, an unkind response to the builders of their 'squatters' home'. In other nests are several pairs of tree sparrows, smaller, more muscular-looking country cousins of the urban, almost domestic house sparrow. Unlike the latter, the sexes are similar in plumage, with an all-brown cap, small black bib and characteristic black spot in the centre of a white cheek distinguishing them from the house sparrow. Their call, a rich fruity chirrup, once heard and learned, is an excellent way of separating the two species at a distance or in flight.

Tree sparrows are just as catholic in their food choices as house sparrows but tend to shun the presence of man, feeding and nesting usually at a distance from human occupation. They normally feed in flocks throughout the year, and nest in rather better-defined colonies than house sparrows. Elsewhere, the nest is often in a hole in a building or tree. The latter case applies to most tree sparrows in the oakwood, where the hole may be a natural one or the disused nest of a woodpecker. Tree sparrows readily occupy nestboxes too, and are unusually pugnacious in their tenancy of them, even evicting other birds like blue or great tits and building their own nest on top of that of the first occupier.

So, by gentle degrees, the pattern that will describe the summer in and around our oak is being established: the chiff-chaff as first migrant to arrive, the oak itself in blossom, the bluebells beneath it; vegetation beginning to flourish again after the shut-down of winter, supporting increasing bird populations already, some of them well advanced in their breeding cycle, supporting, too, a rapidly mounting insect population – but the true summer is the time for them.

*Wood sorrel*

# SUMMER

S summer advances, the bluebell petals wither and fade and the seed pods increase their angular bulk. The yellow archangel, too, has gone, and in the spaces around the oak even the later-flowering and much taller red campion has been swamped by bracken. When it first emerges, dusted with reddish-brown hairs and curled like a bishop's crook, bracken can be a most attractive sight. What is seen above the ground is entirely the leaves and their stalks, as the stems, in the form of rough, tough rhizomes, ramify underground. But this is a plant that has few friends. On heath and moor it perseveres in invading the grass pastures and fields hard-won over the centuries by generations of farmers. Many even is the nature reserve where, once grazing pressure has been removed to encourage the less common plants to flourish, the domineering bracken has insidiously crept in and begun the gradual swamping process.

Flourishing on many soils, in good conditions bracken can easily grow taller than a man, as is the case in many of the glades in the oakwood. Here it harbours a tiny mite, often called the 'bracken bug' but more properly a harvest mite. This mite is a blood sucker, and infests warm-blooded animals, primarily rabbits and in some areas deer. It climbs plant stems and waits to be brushed off on to a passing victim, and man falls perfectly acceptably into this role. Once on the body, the mites – so small as to be invisible without a lens and too small even to tickle (at this stage) – wander about until constrained by a tight layer of clothing. Round the tops of socks and around the waist are typical areas where they then burrow into skin pores in search of a blood meal. While doing so they set up a considerable inflammation, a process which kills them but which provides their unfortunate host with several days of often intolerable itching.

Beneath the oak, the dark-green leathery-leaved dog's mercury can endure the lack of light through most of the summer. In the past this plant was regarded as a medicinal herb, and a tea-like infusion of its dried leaves was drunk to cure ailments as varied as rheumatism, dropsy and intestinal disorders. Another herb, scarce and sporadic in its occurrence, also grows beneath the oaks: this is a blue-riband plant for botanists, called herb Paris. Vaguely similar to dog's mercury, and less than a foot high, its stem is topped by four long leaves set at right-angles, giving it its scientific specific name *quadrifolia*. Above this cross of leaves rises the flower, composed of four green sepals with four spiky off-white petals positioned between them, sometimes topped by a pea-sized spherical black fruit. Although it features in many of the old herbals as a component of homeopathic medicinal preparations (especially in France), modern works strictly forbid its use because of its high potential toxicity. Despite appearances, herb Paris is a member of the lily family, as is another oakwood scarcity (though a common enough cottage garden plant), Solomon's seal. Spear-like shoots break through the soil and leaf litter in April, sending out a gracefully arching shoot a couple of feet long. From this shoot, pairs of neat tubular green-tipped white flowers hang like bells beneath the paired leaves through May and June.

*Solomon's seal*

On the edge of the area beneath the oak shaded by its leaves, a couple
of shrubs, both with many relatives in gardens, grow thoroughly entwined
together. The more upright and robust of them, though not necessarily the
stronger grower, is one of the viburnums, guelder rose. This shrub produces
elder-flower-like panicles of flowers, 3 or 4 inches (7.5–10 cm) across,
through June. Closer inspection shows that much of its showy appearance
is due to the outer ring of purest-white flowers. These indeed *are* strictly
for show: they are sterile and serve only as a glaring attraction for potential
pollinating insects. It is the mass of small greenish inner flowers that will
produce the spectacular clusters of bright scarlet berries in autumn.

The guelder rose's partner is the honeysuckle, wiry, straggling, yet
rampant. The honeysuckle uses its rich scent to attract insect pollinators,
but its tubular flowers – almost trumpet-like – have been fashioned by
evolution to be selective. So long is the tube that only the longer-tongued
moths can reach the rich supply of nectar at the base, and so serve as
pollinators as they press in to reach the nectar. Pick a honeysuckle flower
and chew the base, and even to the relatively insensitive human palate the
unmistakeable perfumed honey-like taste is a delight. As in all walks of life,
however, there are cheats: look clearly at the clusters of blooms and you
will find some with a neat hole punctured in the tube at the base, close by
the nectaries. In all probability this is where one of the much shorter-
tongued nectar-lovers, perhaps a bee, has taken a short cut to the food –
a short cut that will do the plant no good as, of course, pollen will not be
transmitted for cross-fertilization by this means.

In contrast to the spring, when great drifts of bluebells or wood anemones
are characteristic of the still reasonably well-lit woodland floor, most of the
conspicuous summer oakwood flowers appear in small clumps or colonies.
One such under the oak is the butcher's broom, dull
and dark green, with small wide 'leaves' (actually
flattened specialized stems). In the centre of many
will be found the minute thorn-like true leaf. The
axil of this leaf sheltered a small white flower
towards the end of the winter: now this is growing
to a green berry, and some of these berries are
beginning to show shades of yellow and orange on
their way to bold autumn reds. Strangely enough,
this plant too belongs to the lily family.

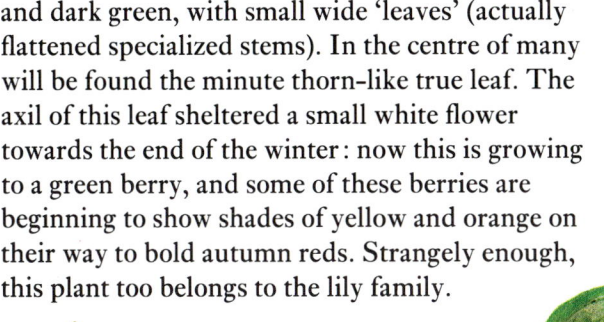

*Herb Paris*

Another showier plant that occasionally grows right under the oak, but more often towards the grassy surrounds where it can bask in occasional sunlight, is the St John's wort. Again familiar to the gardener as various forms of hypericum (like the rose of Sharon), the St John's worts are excellent indicators in oakwoods of the nature of the soil. Three species are involved, each a foot or more high and with yellow flowers. The one typical of the oakwood and to be found under our oak is *Hypericum perforatum*, the perforate St John's wort. This is probably the biggest of the three, and arguably in some ways the showiest, with large pale-yellow flowers with long yellow stamens. As a distinguishing feature, the stem has two prominent ribs, and the presence of this species typifies a good rich neutral loam soil. Were our oak to be on a chalky soil, the ragged and untidy, rather smaller-flowered *Hypericum hirsutum*, the hairy or hoary St John's wort, would be the one growing near it. This has a round stem and plenty of downy hairs on the leaves. In contrast, on acid soils *Hypericum pulchrum* is the indicator plant – the 'red litmus paper' as it were. This is known as the beautiful St John's wort, and beautiful it really is. Smaller and neater than the other two, it has shiny

*St John's wort*

green heart-shaped leaves and richer yellow flowers. In bud these flowers look upright and rather like candles because they are tipped with a glorious flame colour. When open, the same rich colour is to be seen in the stamens, contrasting with the open gold petals. No less a botanist than John Gilmour, then director of the Cambridge University Botanic Garden, described this as the 'loveliest wild flower in Britain'.

Above and around these flowers, and indeed all about the oak, by summer the air is literally buzzing with life. Closer inspection will show, too, that on the oak – its bark, its twigs, its leaves – insects are flourishing. All the different stages may be found, as the population dynamics (and reproductive strategies) of the various insect species vary widely. Thus eggs, larvae, pupae and adult insects (often called 'perfect' forms by Victorian entomologists) are all there to be seen, but not necessarily easily, as many and varied are the techniques they use to avoid their predators, which range in size from microscopic mites, through other insects, to small mammals and birds. These plant-eating insects are a vital link in the life-chains of many animals, including other insects, in the same way that fish, poultry, beef, lamb and pork are to the meat-eating humans: they perform the difficult task of turning plant material into digestible food.

It is said that more than half of the 30,000 or so insect species recorded in Britain depend on deciduous woodland for a living, and among the various native deciduous trees the oak is thought to be the one capable of supporting most species, certainly a total of many thousands of different ones. In contrast to, for example, the birds, mammals and fishes, where a great deal is known about the lives of all the British species (though there are relatively few species to know something about), for the insects, spiders and other arthropods (the woodlice, millipedes and so forth) rather more seems to be known about the numbers and, in general, rather less about their individual life histories.

Shaking or tapping an oak branch over a sheet of paper, or better still over a white-painted board or tray, gives some idea of the numbers involved, and the immense variety of shapes and sizes. For example, the caterpillars of over one hundred different moths have been recorded on oak, one of the two commonest being the green oak tortrix, whose moth is a velvety pale green and just under an inch long. Tortrix caterpillars may occur in huge numbers: they are 'loopers' – moving by humping their back and bringing tail forward to head in a jerky progression – and tend to wriggle violently if disturbed, falling off the leaves in the process. This reaction presumably helps them avoid being eaten by predators. As they fall, they spin a silk 'life-line', and once disturbance has ceased, climb back up to continue feeding. They tend to use silken threads to roll the leaves on which they are feeding into a protective tube or tent. The caterpillars are active as soon as the leaves unfold, and are full-grown in June. They pupate aloft, in a rolled leaf, emerging in July to flutter round the canopy.

Green oak tortrix and the equally numerous winter moth can strip the leaves off twigs and branches, or occasionally whole trees. Most caterpillars cause far less damage. The oak is occasionally attacked by the lackey moth, dumpy-bodied, with a wingspan of an inch or more, and buff or brown with two darker brown bars across the forewings. The adult moths are on the wing during June and July, mostly at night when they are easily attracted to lights. The eggs – like miniature Neopolitan ice-creams – are laid in a cluster at the base of an oakleaf, or at the junction of a twig, and remain there through the winter. In spring they hatch and the caterpillars begin to construct a communal tent-like web. On warm days, they will apparently sun-bathe, basking on the webbing surface, and the tent shelters them as a group, both while feeding and when they cast their skins, which they do

*Lackey moth*

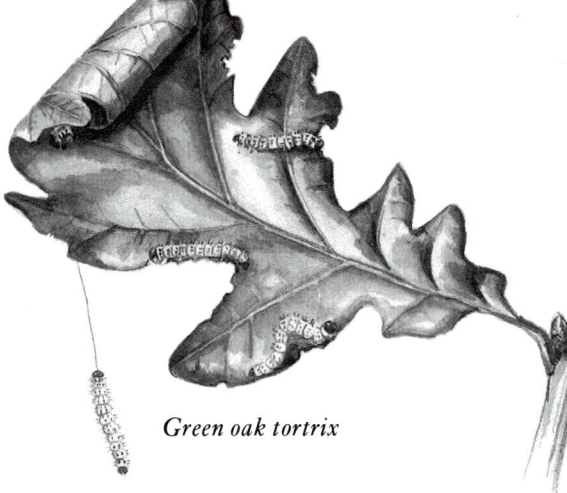

*Green oak tortrix*

several times on the way to maturity.

The lackey moth caterpillar is strikingly coloured, especially as it nears full growth: on the ground colour of French blue are narrow longitudinal stripes of white, orange and black, with orange flecks on the underparts and a series of black velvety blobs at the head and tail ends. The hairs are brown, quite long but sparse enough to allow the beauty of the colours to show clearly. When mature, the caterpillar retreats and pupates, the chrysalis concealed in a loosely woven double-skinned silk cocoon attached by silken threads to the underside of a leaf.

Another moth that sometimes feeds on the oak also feeds in groups, though in this case without the protective tent. Buff-tip caterpillars gather on the undersides of the leaves, often lying with their tail ends close to the leaf mid-rib and their bodies stretched out parallel or even along the side veins of the leaf in orderly array. They are on the oak later in the summer – usually in August and even September – and when full-grown (getting on for 2 inches (5 cm) long) can be an impressive sight. Probably it is their bold yellow colouring with a number of longitudinal dotted black lines down their bodies, the most striking down the centre of the back, that protects them from attack. The colours yellow, orange and red, in combination with black and white, are commonly associated with insect species like the buff-tip moth that are unpalatable to birds. This so-called 'warning colouration' deters birds from attacking them, and interestingly a number of other insects, basically quite edible it seems, have jumped on this evolutionary band-wagon by mimicking the proven protective colour patterns of others!

The adult buff-tip moth is an evening and night-time flyer, only rarely disturbed into flight during the day. Seen in flight by torch-light, it is quite conspicuous, with a 2 inch (5 cm) wingspan and each dove-grey forewing

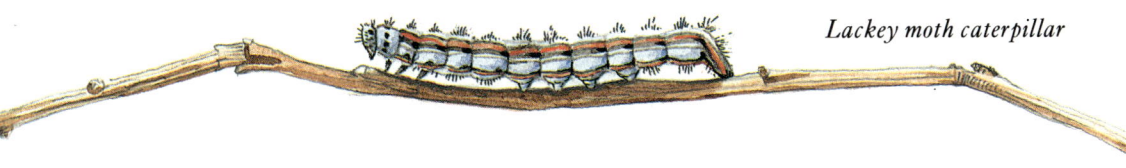

*Lackey moth caterpillar*

tipped with a bold golden-buff blob from which it gets its name. Amazingly, when it lands on the oak trunk, mottled with algae and lichens, it seems almost to vanish without trace, so good is its camouflage. The wings are folded in a ridge along the length of the body rather than held spread (like a butterfly's), which helps this excellent concealment.

Broadly similar in colouration, but smaller and much commoner round the oak (and widespread elsewhere) is the buff footman. This narrow-winged moth is greyish fawn, with a striking golden-buff leading edge to the forewing. Its wingspan is about $1\frac{1}{2}$ inches (4 cm). The moth is about during July, and is often disturbed from among the leaves of the lower branches as you brush past, always quickly darting back into cover. The drab grey-green caterpillars are more difficult to find, however, because in the strictest sense they do not feed on the oak itself. The best place to seek them is on the side of the oak trunk that remains moistest through the summer, where they browse on the green algae that flourish there.

A fair number of moths boast the name 'oak' somewhere in their own. In the case of the spectacular oak eggar, with a huge woolly caterpillar loved as a food source by cuckoos, this can be misleading. A golden-brown moth with a 2 to 3 inch (5–7·5 cm) wingspan, each wing with a paler band and the forewings with a bold white spot, the oak eggar can be seen flying near oakwoods, but its main host plants are smaller shrubs, often those commonly found in hedgerows.

The oak beauty, though, lives up to both parts of its name. Two inches (5 cm) or more in span, its wings are marvellously mottled and shaded, like

*Buff-tip caterpillar*

*Oak beauty*

shot-silk, in whites, greys and buffs, and the male has golden-buff feather-
like antennae. With wings folded, this beauty again turns to competent
camouflage against the oak trunk. Oak beauties fly early in the summer –
normally in March and April, and the greyish-violet looper caterpillars feed
on the oak's foliage between May and July. Occasionally darker forms of
this moth are to be seen. The oak beauty is called scientifically *Biston
strataria*, and considerable research has gone into the life of a close relative,
*Biston betularia*, the peppered moth, which also frequents the oak woodland
and whose caterpillars sometimes feed on oak foliage, among a wide range
of other plants. Dark, or melanic, forms of the peppered moth are often
quite numerous, so the colour range is from bright white with black spots
and chequers through to grey with darker markings. The occurrence of
darker forms increases dramatically in woodland areas close to industrial
conurbations. The research showed that the darker forms, when at rest on
the grimy tree trunks close to smoky factories, survived better than the paler
ones because their camouflage protected them so much better against their
predators, which are mainly birds. We tend to think of evolution as a
process taking aeons of time, but here is a neat example of the flexibility
of the process and its potential speed of response to rapidly changing
modern circumstances.

Also black and white, but rather larger and less variable in hue, is the
leopard moth. The male has a pale-grey body with black-spotted white
wings spanning just over 1 inch (2·5 cm). The female is dark-grey-bodied,
but has similar wing patterns. She is appreciably larger (as is quite often
the case with moths) with a wingspan exceeding 2 inches (5 cm). In the past
the oak and other trees in the wood have suffered at the hands – or rather
the mouthparts – of leopard moth caterpillars. The foliage, however, has
escaped, as the leopard moth larva burrows into the smaller branches.
Reaching a couple of inches in length, the moth is safe in its burrow from
all save woodpeckers and parasitic wood-boring wasps. It takes two or even
three years to reach pupation. Often enough, those twigs or branches
hollowed out by leopard moths will break off under the strain of a strong
gust of wind from an unfamiliar quarter, and several of the smaller scars
in the oak's canopy arose in this way.

Amongst this legion of moths likely at some time or another to be
associated with the oak are many small species – the *Microlepidoptera* –
mostly an undistinguished mottled brown in colour and often very difficult
to identify. Larger, but just as drab, is the lobster moth. Looking at it, grey-
brown, with darker and paler flecks and streaks, it is difficult to see how
on earth it got its name. Every so often it lays its tiny hemispherical eggs
on the oak. The caterpillar emerges usually in July, and feeds on the leaves

*Lobster moth caterpillar*

until it pupates in September, the chrysalis concealed in a tightly-woven silken cocoon spun between a couple of dead or dying leaves. Caterpillars come in many shapes, sizes and colours, but the lobster moth's must take the prize for sheer grotesqueness. For the first few days of its life, the tiny caterpillar is thought to feed only on its own eggshell, but it soon moults and starts to feed and grow normally.

Red-brown in colour, it adopts an extraordinary posture if disturbed, presumably to deter any bird keen on taking it for a quick snack. The bulbous head rears up and back from the twig that the caterpillar is clasping, the long legs on the front segments folded almost like those of a preying mantis. The caterpillar retains its grip with the suckers on the 'false' legs on the segments back towards its tail, but the tail segments themselves, swollen and with conspicuous pale stripes, are arched forward menacingly over the back. This rather scorpion-like pose is further enhanced by two long appendages on the final segment, resembling the scorpion's sting. When the caterpillar is well grown, an inch or more long, this must prove a rather daunting and aggressive-looking adversary for the small canopy-feeding birds like tits and warblers.

Strangely, though so many moths are closely allied with the oak, the same cannot be said for the butterflies. Through the oakwood as a whole, and particularly in the more sheltered glades between big clumps of oaks, many butterflies are to be seen on warm summer days. Earliest to appear, sometimes while the oak is in flower and before its leaves have emerged, are the beautiful pale sulphur-yellow brimstone and the diminutive and delicate orange-tip. The source of the latter's name is obvious in the male, but the female, with grey wing-tip patches, looks like a small type of white butterfly. Orange-tips often flight back and forth over plants like charlock, hedge mustard and garlic mustard, and their larvae feed on these and on another plant among those first to flower in the spring, the pink cuckoo-flower, lady's smock or milkmaids (to give just a few of its many names).

The ginger-brown crinkle-edged comma, named after the white mark of that shape on its wings, is conspicuous when the bramble tangles are in flower, while peacock, red admiral and small tortoiseshell frequent the beds of nettles. These familiar butterflies, together with the various browns, blues and coppers, are typical countryside creatures, perhaps more numerous along hedgerows and over old flower-rich meadows, but able to survive well in the oakwood glades. Others, like the speckled wood and marbled white, though feeding as caterpillars on plants like grasses and vetches, seem to prefer the shade offered by woodland when flying free as adult butterflies.

One of the most elegant of butterflies, outdoing even the red admiral for size, is the purple emperor. Nowhere common, this grand velvet-brown butterfly, the male alone suffused with a metallic purple sheen, lays its eggs on the sallows away down in the damper parts of the wood. Here the larvae mature and pupate, feeding on sallow, but once the adults are flying they may visit the oak. Often enough, the oak is their main habitat through July and part of August. They flit gracefully round the upper reaches of the canopy – binoculars are a useful aid here if you want to watch them closely – and often pause to rest or to feed among the leaves. Strangely enough, the food that they seek on the oak leaves is the honeydew, that sugar-rich fluid excreted by the masses of aphids colonizing the oak shoots. Only rarely will purple emperors come down to ground level, and then in gruesome circumstances. They, like some others of their kind, find the fluids given off by the stinking, decomposing carcase of a rabbit or hedgehog a valuable food source, rich in proteins. In days past when butterfly collecting and killing was in vogue, the 'specimen' being pinned out, wings spread, on a display board, the purple emperor – because of its high-flying habits – was regarded as an extremely difficult quarry. The old collectors overcame their problem by baiting the purple emperors down to some rotting meat.

As fate would decree, the one butterfly really to be linked, life-through, to the oak is also a high-flyer and also has 'purple' in its name. It is the purple hairstreak, its upper wing surfaces dark brown with a purple sheen especially on the forewings. The hindwings each have a stubby protrusion, like a miniature swallow-tail. The underside is grey-brown with paler bands, with a dark-centred orange eyespot on the hindwings. Not much over an inch in wingspan, the purple hairstreak flits around the canopy through July and August, feeding for much of the time on aphid honeydew. At this time, the oak is forming the buds from which its next season's shoots will grow, and around these buds the female purple hairstreak lays her eggs. These hatch as the buds burst in the following spring, allowing the young caterpillars, brown and furry, an opportunity to feed well before their tannin content gets too high. The larva pupates in late May or early June, either beneath a leaf or in the leaf litter beneath the tree.

Although again not *strictly* directly dependent on the oak, the heath fritillary, one of the scarcest, and increasingly threatened, of our butterflies, is often seen in its vicinity. The rather bare areas of ground beneath the tree are inhospitable terrain for most plants, but one strange one that can and does survive is the cow-wheat. This is a rather fragile-looking annual, its narrow leaves set in opposing pairs and often brown-tinged, with small tubular yellow flowers. Straggling, and rarely more than a few inches high, the cow-wheat seems always at risk of being overwhelmed. As it is an annual, it may of course not appear in the same place in successive years – much will depend on how much seed was set and how far it dispersed. This poses something of a problem for the heath fritillary, a black-blotched ginger-brown butterfly with a wingspan of about 2 inches (5 cm), darker above than many fritillaries, but with the usual ginger and white chequerboard pattern on the underwings.

The adults are on the wing in May (it has been called the 'May fritillary') and the slender, ribbed eggs that they lay hatch in July. After feeding for a few weeks, the caterpillars hibernate together in a silken protective canopy, emerging the following spring to continue to feed and grow quickly, pupating in May. Perhaps it is the vagaries of appearance of its food plant, the cow-wheat, or perhaps other factors such as changing climate may be playing a role, but the heath fritillary is becoming steadily scarcer and is restricted to fewer and fewer oakwoods in the south of Britain.

But what of the myriad other sorts of insects, many representatives of which will have fallen on to the beating tray? There will be mites – not insects, but round-bodied and microscopic, with four pairs of legs. Most mites are slow-moving, so slow on the beating tray that you have to look twice to be sure that your eyes are not playing tricks; but others, some of them red, flabby and velvety, others pale brown, move much more quickly. These are predators, depending on speed to catch other mites or small insects, and then using piercing mouthparts, sucking the body contents from them.

Other predators are to be seen as well, some well-known like the various ladybirds, voracious feeders on aphid colonies and with larvae which, looked at through a hand lens, appear for all the world like microscopic dinosaurs. Perhaps more surprising are insects like earwigs, well able to eat plant material but also with a liking for the eggs and larvae of small insects; and lacewings, probably both green and brown, delicate looks belying their savage habits. Lacewing eggs are laid in clusters, each one atop a long flexible stalk to keep them out of reach of still other predators!

As a general rule (and for obvious reasons) predators run faster than their prey, so a first inspection of what has fallen on to the beating tray will show a number of caterpillars, a moth or two, and numerous aphids, all almost stationary, while among them other insects – the predators – dash about nimbly. Often commonest amongst them are $\frac{1}{4}$ inch (6 mm) long, slender, green capsid bugs, whose clearly visible, long, tubular mouthparts seem ideally adapted to spearing aphids and sucking the juice from them. Some are also plant-sap feeders, which is the main means of feeding of their larger and much broader relatives, the aptly-named shield bugs. Another family of bugs often featuring are the anthocorids, rather smaller than the capsids and chequered black and white. These are valuable members of the farming community, too, because in orchard and hop garden (as in the canopy of the oak) they can help to maintain a balance by keeping harmful insects like aphids restricted to tolerable numbers. Each year, the surplus numbers from the oak tend to migrate out into the surrounding countryside: they are catholic in their choice of diet and often visit gardens, not even being averse to biting the gardener!

Spiders, too, are often abundant: on the oak leaves (especially when they are still pale green) the most numerous is a delicate pale-green species of *Araneus*, which spins a small orb web between the leaves to ensnare flying insects like aphids and fruit flies. Others, like the green and brown crab spider, *Diaea dorsata* (shaped like a miniature crab), prefer to lie in wait amongst the leaves, jumping out on any prey that comes within reach and quickly immobilizing it with venom injected as it bites.

Other insects well-prepared to attack man (and other mammals) lurk beneath the oak, or shelter in its foliage. Though reared in stagnant water, often some considerable distance away, mosquitoes will whine forth from among the leaves within instants of their sophisticated sensory system alerting them to the presence of a warm-blooded animal. For the female mosquito particularly, this means the chance of a blood meal, vital if she is to be successful in reaching the egg-laying stage of her life. Mosquitoes have a very light touch: skilful in flight, they can alight on a human arm unnoticed, and so scalpel-sharp are the minute blades of their mouthparts (which work rather like an electric carving knife) that even their bite is often not felt until it is too late. By then, the anti-coagulants that they inject to keep the blood flowing freely for drinking will have caused a reactionary swelling, with immediate pain and subsequent irritation and itching.

If mosquitoes operate with the delicacy of touch of a surgeon with a hypodermic needle, horseflies, in contrast, display all the finesse of road workers wielding pneumatic drills. Like the mosquitoes, these are members of the fly family, or Diptera (meaning two-winged), but they are shaped much more on the lines of the domestic blowfly, and some horseflies are even bulkier than a good-sized bluebottle. Horsefly mouthparts are blunt and crude compared with those of a mosquito and in consequence their bite is often detected right at the outset and before any harm is done. If not, then they too can cause painful swellings. The larvae – whitish maggots – are raised in the damp soil beneath the oak, where they feed on other insect larvae and small soil animals. The commonest horsefly, often called a clegg, is almost ½ inch (12 mm) long and brownish, but others show green or gold body patterns. All have the most striking eyes: as in insects in general, these are compound – that is made up of a honeycomb of many very tiny lenses – but in the horseflies they are huge, and often glitter like oildrops with refracted light. So large are they that the two take up virtually the whole frontal area of the head, giving the horsefly the appearance of a small helicopter with a perspex 'blister' cabin. Ranging far and wide among the trees, the larger ones often flying with an audible buzz, horseflies too are quick to sense the higher temperature of a warm-blooded mammal and head towards it with enthusiasm and persistence too if the man or animal tries to drive them away.

*Horsefly*

Various beetles will usually be represented in the beating-tray 'catch', and if beating is carried out at regular intervals through the summer there is a wonderful fascination in seeing how both numbers and species change as the season progresses. Members of the beetle family have chewing mouthparts, and among the more conspicuous ones likely to be encountered on the oak are several weevils, usually less than ½ inch (12 mm) long and recognizable because of their bulbous body and long narrow 'nose', like an elephant's trunk but sprouting a pair of antennae about halfway along. Weevils tend to chew semi-circular scallops out of the margins of the leaves.

Another distinctive group of beetles often found in the oak are the wood-borers. These tend to be cylindrical in shape, of much the same diameter all the way from front to rear, and to have very reduced legs tucked away out of sight, all features that would be expected in a beetle that tunnels beneath the bark. It is these that produce the 'woodworm' or 'shot holes' neatly drilled into the occasional stump of a dead branch on the oak, and they and their relatives are notorious for giving the owners of old timber-framed houses and wooden furniture such a shock when little piles of fine sawdust are found beneath their neatly-drilled circular tunnel entrances. By far the largest and most spectacular of the beetles likely (although only rarely) to be encountered near the oak is the stag beetle. Occasionally a full-grown male will exceed 2 inches (5 cm) in length, about one third of this being accounted for by the pair of giant 'antlers' into which parts of its mouthparts have been converted. The antlers are reddish-brown, and the beetle's back has a purple sheen: it is relatively long-legged, with long, jointed antennae ending in tiny bushes. Thus even to man it may seem a fearsome creature, but the jaws are so huge and cumbersome that the male stag beetle can only administer a gentle pinch: his jaw muscles just cannot manage anything stronger. In some ways like their mammal counterparts, the males use their 'antlers' in display, occasionally indulging in head-to-head wrestling bouts. The female stag beetle is rather smaller in the body and has much smaller jaws with which she *can* administer a painful nip.

The eggs are laid in decaying wood, most often in a branch stump or in a fallen bough (usually several inches in diameter) lying and rotting slowly away beneath the oak. The full-grown larva is the size of a cocktail sausage, waxy white with a ginger-brown head capsule, and takes two or three years to reach maturity.

Relatively rarely will a stag beetle be found up in the oak's foliage. Probably the largest insect likely to be seen among the leaves will be one of the longhorn grasshoppers or, as they are more properly called, bush crickets. Only infrequently do these bush crickets, with their very long antennae sweeping back well beyond their tails, take to the wing – indeed, some species cannot fly. The largest, which is occasionally to be seen in the oak, is the great green bush cricket, whose length can exceed 2 inches (5 cm). Like its relatives, but unlike the true grasshoppers, it usually crawls rather than hops, despite its apparently powerful back legs. Common every year on the oak is the pale leaf-green oak bush cricket, around 1 inch (2·5 cm) long, fairly slender in the body, the female with a conspicuous scimitar-shaped ovipositor at the tip of her tail. However fearsome this organ may seem, it will never give you a sting! It is used purely to bury her eggs below the ground.

While grasshoppers out in the open glades are at their most active and noisy during the heat of the summer day, it is not until the evening that the bush crickets start to become active. Both families have chewing mouthparts of complex structure, and are quite fascinating to watch as they nibble away at the margin of a leaf or at an aphid – which, when left alone, they quickly settle down to do. The grasshoppers are primarily vegetarian, but the bush crickets seem to concentrate mainly on animal matter, especially slow-moving insects with little chance of escape, like the wingless aphid colonies.

Crickets and grasshoppers fall into the category of 'more often heard than seen', and their rasping calls are well-known to everyone. These calls, or 'song', are made by a process called 'stridulation' when two parts of the body are rubbed together, a highly miniaturized version of a child running a ruler along some railings. In the grasshoppers the 'file' is on the legs and the 'scraper' on the wings, while in the bush crickets one is on the left wing, the other on the right. To 'sing', both wings are raised over the back and rubbed together, emitting a high-pitched long-drawn-out drone. This noise

*Bush cricket*

is received, or 'heard', by a vibration-sensitive spot (which can hardly be called an ear) on the foreleg. Coming out of the oak, this rather strident song will usually emanate from the great green, as the oak bush cricket is something of an exception to its relatives in being silent.

While some insects or their larvae resort to camouflage to protect themselves against predators large and small, and others resort to bright warning colouration, yet others take refuge *within* the oak while they feed. The leopard moth caterpillar is one such, but much more numerous are those insect larvae that tunnel through the leaf tissue. Hardly surprisingly, these insects do not feature on the beating tray, but in most years their presence on the oak is detectable, even with a cursory glance at the lower leaves, from early summer onwards.

Given the vulnerability of the insects feeding *on* the leaves to predators, it is perhaps not surprising to find that this habit, called 'leaf mining', is widespread through a number of insect orders. The thinness of the leaf blade, or lamina, has imposed structural peculiarities that are common to all the larvae that mine: in general the legs are lost or much reduced and the body is flattened from top to bottom. The mines themselves are often characteristic of their creators, but two groups are easily distinguishable, 'serpentine' (sometimes called 'gallery') and 'blotch'. To a large degree these names are self-explanatory. Mines formed by the blotch miners on the oak show up as irregularly shaped pale patches where the larva (in this case usually one of the oak weevils) has browsed around, eating out the chlorophyll-containing cells between the upper and lower leaf cuticles. Serpentine mines, as the name implies, snake about on the leaf surface, sometimes the upper, sometimes the lower. From a tiny pin-point start (where the egg was laid or the larva originally invaded) the mine wanders about the leaf, leaving a whitish trail gradually increasing in width (as the larva 'digging' it grows) until it reaches an exit hole. In the case of most of those on the oak, there is also sometimes a pupating chamber at the end of the tunnel, where the larva metamorphoses (usually it is one of the tiny microlepidopterous moths), before emerging.

Some thirty species of Microlepidoptera mine in the leaves of oak in Britain, often several occurring on the same tree, but perhaps more striking is that, even within this apparently secure microhabitat, their predators have sought them out. An amazing fifteen species of small parasitic wasps – with ovipositors long enough to penetrate the leaf and reach the moth larva within its mine, and to lay their egg *inside* the larva which the developing wasp destroys as it grows – have been recorded in one detailed study of the parasites of just two species of oak-mining moths.

Not only will late March have brought the first migrant chiff-chaff of the year to sing in the oak, but it will also have allowed one of the songsters in the wood, whose song is so fragile as to be drowned when the full choir of summer gets going at full blast, to be heard. April is the same, and an afternoon watching the oak should reveal a treecreeper, whose song is a descending high-pitched spindly trill and final flourish. It is said to be a sure sign of increasing age when the naturalist's eardrum loses its sensitivity to these high-frequency notes. It is at this time of the year that treecreeper pairs display: a novel performance as the birds chase each other in spirals up the oak's trunk, calling excitedly with their shrill 'tseeet' – a characteristic note throughout the year.

Treecreepers are brown above, with various darker and paler streaks, and off-white below. In good lighting conditions and during dry weather, this white can appear almost silvery, shading to fawn on the flanks, but in damp weather, when the belly has been pressed close against the lichen-covered bark of the oak, it can appear brownish or even greenish. The tail is long and brown, the wings short and rounded, with a conspicuous pale crescentic wingbar visible in flight. Seen climbing spirally up the trunk, treecreepers look almost like slender mice, but observed in flight, which is deeply undulating and rather feeble, they appear much dumpier and almost moth-like, so rounded are the wings.

The usual nest site, used year after year, is behind a peeling flap of bark, perhaps 6 inches (15 cm) or so across and an inch or two clear of the oak's trunk. In this narrow slit, the boat-shaped nest

*Treecreeper*

of fine twigs is lodged and the eggs laid. Not only is there a 'front door' slit entrance, but an 'emergency exit' above and behind the nest too – a sensible precaution for the sitting female to avoid marauding predators like squirrels and weasels. The very nature of the nest site under rotten bark, and the tenuous nature of the nest supports, mean that great care must be taken when inspecting the nest. Perhaps the best technique is to use a small torch and either a dentist's mirror or a fragment of hand mirror mounted at an angle on a short holder: then the bark flap need not be touched at all.

Treecreepers feed mostly on small insects, spiders and other bark-living invertebrate animals and their eggs and larvae. Their long, slender and very finely pointed down-curved beaks must be ideal for extracting such tiny items from the crevices in the bark in which they are hidden. The eyes are large and protected by unusually 'beetling' eyebrows for a small, slow-flying land bird. The purpose of these is obscure, but a close-up view through binoculars will reveal that they give to the otherwise docile-seeming treecreeper an extremely bad-tempered expression, emphasized additionally by the long, bold, white eyestripe.

The stiff tail of the treecreeper resembles a woodpecker's, with the shafts of the central feathers specially strengthened. As in the case of the woodpecker (to which treecreepers are not related) the tail is used as a prop, the treecreeper too always moving head-uppermost on the trunk or branches of the oak. This is a case of 'parallel evolution', where two unrelated birds have arrived at the same anatomical solution to their problems.

Superficially the nuthatch too looks like a sort of small woodpecker, so similar are its movements on a tree trunk. But notice that the nuthatch scrambles about just as easily head-down as head-up on the oak trunk. Unlike the woodpecker family and the treecreeper, with specially strong central tail feathers, the nuthatch has a soft tail and can move in any direction.

Nuthatches seem to prefer the mature or aged oaks in the wood, and decrepit trees seem to exercise a special fascination. This must be because of the feeding possibilities on offer. Although they do take insects and their larvae, particularly in summer, nuthatches specialize in nuts. Larger and harder ones, like acorns from the oak and beechmast and hazel nuts from elsewhere in the wood, are carried in the beak to a suitable (and regularly used) crevice in the bark of one of the thickest horizontal branches of the oak and hammered open with the beak. This characteristic hammering is one of the best ways of locating the birds in winter.

In spring nuthatches are very noisy, their ringing monosyllabic calls and trilling song being far-carrying. The elaborate but usually concealed black and white patterns beneath the tail and under the wings are used during the short display season, both birds of the pair taking advantage of an exposed, long-dead branch in the crown of the oak for this purpose. Once nesting is under way the birds are quiet and secretive: they nest in holes or cavities in the oaks, often far larger than necessary, flooring the nest chamber, characteristically, with flakes of dry bark. Another distinctive quality of nuthatches' nests is the liberal plastering of mud that seems part of the essential pattern of the life of this species. Over-sized entrance holes are plastered round inside to reduce them to the correct diameter. They may use astonishing quantities of mud, sometimes even a couple of pounds or more in weight, collected by the beakful from the banks of a stream.

For many of the birds that feed around the oak and specialize in insect catching, it is the sheer volume of food that the oak shelters that they find so attractive – the type or commonness of any particular species has relatively little importance as long as the overall richness remains high. Thus the treecreepers continue to patrol the trunk and branches, while chiff-chaff and willow warbler (and, in western oakwoods, the wood warbler too) flit through the canopy taking insects off leaf and twig, sometimes hovering in the process, pecking aphids off the underside of an otherwise inaccessible leaf. Sometimes the warblers will sally forth after flying insects, but in the main this technique is the province of the spotted flycatcher (and, again in wetter western oaks, the pied flycatcher).

The most conspicuous of the oak insects – at least in terms of visual spectacle – are the caterpillars of the winter moth. These are early-summer grazers on the oak leaves, perforating them while they are still soft and yellow-green and low in the tannins that come with dark-green leathery maturity, serving as an effective deterrent to insect feeding. Often the caterpillar numbers are sufficient only to increase the green lace-like effect of the leaves against the sky, but sometimes even a tree as majestic as the oak can be near enough defoliated by the insect hordes. Such devastation has on occasion happened to the oak, but such is its stature that later leaves have been able to function effectively enough to ensure its survival to the next season, and rarely do such severe attacks occur in successive seasons.

When caterpillar numbers are high, and the caterpillars themselves well-grown, they can be heard on a still afternoon, munching in their millions, their frass, or droppings, pattering down on to the dry leaf litter below with a sound like gentle drizzling rain. As they mature, the caterpillars lower themselves to the ground on threads of silk to pupate in the soil surface.

This massive, if short-lived, 'crop' of caterpillars is of vital importance to blue and great tits, besides its all-round usefulness to any other insect-eating bird or even small mammals. The young tits, and indeed the success of the whole tit population, are closely dependent on the size of the winter moth caterpillar crop on the oaks and on the timing of the caterpillar hatch. Usually, and most mysteriously, both the timing of laying by the tits, and the size of the clutch, is pretty well correlated to the caterpillar crop and its timing – how the tits know in advance what to expect, and when, is difficult to imagine. It may be that a combination of winter temperatures, spring day length, spring temperatures and perhaps other factors govern both tits and winter moths, but the value of the close tie-up is illustrated abundantly clearly when the system fails. Walking through the wood in such a season when there are young tits in their nests, you can hear the anxious, hungry, shrill piping for food, and find families cold and dead, purely from starvation, in nests where they were flourishing a few days before. A predator may hear, better than you can, the cries of the young tits, and as a very capable tree climber the weasel is quickly up to the nest. He can easily manage to climb through the hole, and a very messy butchery ensues.

But we are getting ahead of ourselves. The tit family in general are great opportunists when it comes to selecting a nest site. Almost any hollow or crevice will suffice, including holes in banks, stone walls and around houses even in such unlikely surrounds as postboxes (little-used ones, presumably) and drainpipes (best in dry summers). Tits are avid users of man-made sites like nestboxes, but in the oak it is either the odd natural cavity – where a branch has broken away and some of the timber has rotted – or the semi-natural sites – the couple of nest chambers excavated by woodpeckers in previous years – that they use. Sometimes it will be blue tits, sometimes great, but rarely both, because they make quarrelsome neighbours when the nests of the two species are in quite such close proximity.

Nest building may start in late March with the collection of a few pieces of moss, but during April it gets under way in earnest. Occasionally great tits will occupy large holes better suited to little owls or stock doves, and on one occasion a pair collected nearly a cubic foot of moss to fill an owl nestbox to an acceptable level, and to bring the nest cup itself – tiny and lost in an expanse of 'filling' – near to the entrance hole. In the oak the first foundations are usually pure moss, or there may be a framework of dead grass or rootlets. Certainly in the wood there is abundant moss, very loose, for collection and the main bulk of the nest is made of it. Usually in a corner of the cavity a 'cup' is formed loosely in the moss, perhaps $1\frac{1}{2}$ inches (4 cm) across. At this time the female starts to lay her eggs — usually before the process of lining the nest is properly under way.

Both great and blue tits lay an egg a day, and almost inevitably the female will conceal the eggs in the loose nest fabric until the clutch is nearly complete, when the eggs will be rooted out and gathered together in the cup. During laying both birds, but especially the male, will have been busy gathering the nest lining – soft and insulating. In the case of the blue tit, the lining is usually of feathers, and the regularity of this allows a preliminary identification of the nest even before the adults are seen. The feathers are usually obtained from corpses, and tend to be from the leftovers of fox kills – usually woodpigeon or pheasant, the former with lots of snow-white down, the latter less practical (because of poorer insulation properties) but more attractive because of its rich colouration and metallic sheen. The great tit, in contrast, generally lines its nest cup with animal hairs: sometimes sheep's wool or cattle hairs collected off barbed wire (rarely horsehair nowadays), but more often tufts of fur from dead rabbits or from fighting hares are used. Occasionally a source of fox fur is found: peering in, it is abundantly obvious when this is the case because the fur retains the characteristic, and not pleasant, persistent odour of foxes. Perhaps it is just as well that birds have little or no sense of smell, because the youngsters keep the taint for a while after they have left the nest.

Even early in the season, the dependence of the tits on the winter moth caterpillars becomes strikingly evident. To get into peak condition for egg laying as early as possible (research has shown that, in general, the nestlings in early broods are both larger in number and healthier), the female must eat prodigiously. Over ten or twelve days she will be producing almost her own weight in eggs, laying one each day. In the three weeks before laying begins, she puts on weight at an extraordinary rate, increasing her weight by at least one half again and sometimes almost doubling it. This she cannot achieve alone, and the male can often be seen hunting and then returning to her side with a beakful of caterpillars that she accepts with her wings fluttering rapidly. This behaviour, called 'courtship feeding', used to be regarded as a gesture to cement the pair bond, as in human terms when gifts of flowers or chocolates serve the same function. The more prosaic explanation, that she must have this additional food to get into breeding condition, lacks charm but it is good evolutionary sense.

It seems logical to suppose that, as they nest in holes, the tit family should be safer from predators than most other small birds. Surprisingly, this is not the case. Perhaps largely because of the need to synchronize the maximum food demands of their brood of youngsters with the single short-lived peak in their caterpillar food supply, great and blue tits have evolved to produce a single large brood of young each year, rather than follow the pattern of most small birds which have two or three broods and thus two or three chances should anything go wrong. Almost literally a case of the tits putting all their eggs in one basket! Thus if a clutch of eggs or a brood of young is lost, although sometimes there is a chance for a fresh start, the late replacement brood is unlikely to be very successful.

The arithmetic of predation is fascinating (if gruesome) and in the oakwood the tits allow a simple demonstration of how this aspect of population dynamics works. Broadly speaking, research has shown that in spring each pair of tits contains one adult bird (which bred the year before and is at least twenty-one months old) and one young bird (about nine months old and breeding for the first time). Thus, in theory, half of each breeding pair dies each year or, in technical terms, adult mortality is fifty per cent. For the tit population to remain at a steady level, all that is necessary is that one youngster be raised, per pair, to replace the adult which has died. For great and blue tits, it is quite fair to work on an average brood size of ten youngsters leaving the nest in the summer. By the following spring, this means that nine of the ten must die, to human eyes

*Blue tits*

a staggering ninety per cent mortality. But this is nature's way of guarding against catastrophe, and quite normal in the bird world. Indeed, were one *extra* youngster to survive each year, it would be only a very few years before the countryside was over-run by hordes of tits which would quickly eat themselves out of house and home and precipitate a disastrous crash in the population, with far more damaging long-term implications.

Obviously 'natural causes' loom large in this high mortality rate, especially starvation and hypothermia due to the difficulties inexperienced young birds have in finding food in winter. But the predators do play a significant part, and may account for one third or more of the deaths. The range of predators is small, but unexpected and interesting. At the start of the season, competition for nesting holes is fierce as there are rarely too many sites. Larger birds such as starlings may oust tits from the bigger holes, and tit may oust tit from smaller ones: the larger great tit does not always succeed in evicting the smaller but more aggressive blue tit. Tree sparrows can squeeze through an entrance apparently only just large enough for a blue tit, and often build their untidy nests on top of a clutch of tit eggs or, as tree sparrows are late nesters, even on top of a flourishing brood of tit youngsters. The tits, of course, do not survive. Great spotted woodpeckers have a taste for tit eggs and young besides their normal insect food, and of course can easily open up the nest hole with a few chisel blows from their beaks. As described earlier, woodpeckers find it relatively easy to take young tits from the nest because they jump up to the nest entrance when they see what they believe to be a parent's shadow falling across it.

Strangely fieldmice, and sometimes voles, will climb trees readily, and equally readily will enjoy the eggs from any bird nests they encounter, the tits being no exception. The prime predatory mammal, however, is the weasel. Well able to squeeze through the nest hole, a weasel will quickly kill all within. Often it will gorge itself to such an extent that it must sleep off its meal until it slims down enough to squeeze out again.

Among the bird predators, although the resident little owl pair may occasionally catch a tit, as do the winter-visiting long-eared owls, it is the sparrowhawk, fast returning to its old good numbers, that is the main threat. In the few weeks after fledging, when the tits' young – particularly those of the great tit which are larger and thus make a better meal – are still mastering the skills of flight, many may fall victim to the sparrowhawks. It is the male sparrowhawk which takes the greatest toll. He is appreciably smaller than his mate but perhaps nimbler in flight, darting through the trunks and branches, and even the canopy twigs, as if they were open air.

Towards the end of summer in the wood, the several parties of tits – usually of various species, with blue and great predominating but marsh, willow, coal and long-tailed often also present – each of a few family groups, may coalesce into flocks sometimes hundreds strong. As they move through the oaks these draw like a magnet – or better, like a whirlpool – other species feeding nearby including wrens, treecreepers, goldcrests and various members of the warbler family.

From the oak tree's point of view, and perhaps also from that of the birds feeding in it, the winter moth must be of singular importance. In Britain there are two species on oak – the winter moth and the northern winter moth. Apart from a geographical distribution difference indicated by their names, the two are closely similar to look at and thus difficult to separate. Even their habits are much the same. The males are grey-buff, with forewings darker and showing a pattern of dark bands barely visible on the hindwings. Their wingspan is about 1 inch (2.5 cm), and (as is so commonly the case with northern animals) the northern winter moth has a slightly greater wingspan than its southern counterpart. The first moths emerge in October from pupae in the soil beneath the oak, and the majority will have emerged by early December. Through these early winter months, they can be seen flying both by day and by night through the oaks, and they are frequent visitors to a torch or a Tilley lamp if one is taken into the oakwood.

But this is only the males. The females are strikingly different: for a start they are wingless, and thus naturally flightless. They have brown, rather podgy bodies less than $\frac{1}{2}$ inch (12 mm) long, and are difficult indeed to spot against the oak's trunk, moving upwards like a rather sluggish spider. On emerging from their chrysalids in the upper layer of soil and leaf litter, they laboriously head for the trunk of the oak and begin to clamber slowly upwards. As they go, they emit (as do most moths) a powerful attractant scent, called a pheromone, which draws in males and mating takes place. These pheromones waft downwind from the female on the tree and, although obviously extremely dilute, they are detectable by the males often at a range of hundreds of yards. One prime reason for the fern-frond-like appearance of the antennae of male moths in general (against the simpler, smaller structures of the female) is that this shape makes them better able to trap and identify the molecules of sex-attractant scent in the air currents.

After she has been fertilized, the female climbs on ever upwards until she lays her eggs, singly or in small groups, among clusters of buds at the ends of twigs or in crevices in the bark nearby. Pale green when laid, the eggs soon change to a brownish-orange which helps to camouflage them from the prying eyes of, for example, blue tits acrobatically examining each bud cluster on a number of occasions through the winter, seeking just such items as much-needed food.

Come late spring and the gradual bursting of the oak buds, the caterpillars hatch. Tiny at first, they are olive-green with black heads. As they grow older, they become brighter green and pale stripes appear along their sides. Most caterpillars hatch during April, and feed until late May or early June, when at about $\frac{3}{4}$ inch (18 mm) long, they descend to the woodland floor on a long silken thread. On reaching the soil they burrow a short distance underground and pupate, undergoing those still poorly understood but seemingly magical changes that transform the plump caterpillar into the delicate adult moth.

The caterpillars that hatch earliest may well beat the first of the leaves to open. In this case, rather than setting off on foot to find food, they spin a short silken thread and wait for a gust of wind to break it and drift them off, like microscopic balloonists, in search of eatable leaves. Occasionally the caterpillars will spin silk to weave leaves together as do the tortricid larvae, but more often they just set about the young growth in voracious hordes, eating all the green parts of the leaves. Early in the season, damage can be both considerable and conspicuous, giving the leaves a lace-like appearance. In really severe attacks, the oak can be almost totally defoliated, but this is a rare occurrence. Nor should it be assumed that the oak 'takes it all lying down', as it were. The tannins contained in the oak leaves form complex chemical relationships with the digestive enzymes of the caterpillar, inhibiting their effectiveness and reducing its rate of growth. Tannins are almost absent from the pale-green just-opened leaves, but increase during the season, and as the leaves turn to darker green they become unpalatable. So, depending on the season, the oak will reduce caterpillar damage using its inbuilt chemical defences.

On the other side of the coin, those caterpillars that hatch early, and are thus sure of a full growth span of fresh eatable leaves, run the gauntlet of being washed off the tree by rain. Early in the season, the weather is unpredictable, the showers heavy, and the part-opened buds offer little by way of protection for the tiny caterpillars against the elements.

So our oak is reasonably well protected against the attacks of winter moths and other defoliating caterpillars: the early invaders risk high mortality due to the weather, and latecomers fail to flourish because of the oak's own chemical-warfare defence, the tannins. Should all else fail, and much of the primary-shoot leaf-growth be stripped, the tree has its second spate of leaf growth – the so-called 'Lammas shoots' that burst forth late in the summer – to rely on for photosynthesis and to produce food for winter survival. There is even an additional sting in the tail of this defence, as the shoots that have been stripped of leaves in one year set relatively few buds, so that next season there is a much poorer caterpillar food supply and in consequence higher winter moth mortality.

From May to August, the wood will have the joy of a constant
background murmur of turtle dove song. Absolutely characteristic of warm
afternoons and evenings, the steady, monotonous purring continues,
confusing the observer trying to locate the singing male. The sound is far-
carrying and slightly ventriloquial, and often there are so many pairs that
the air seems to be made of purring. Every so often, a male will climb up
from the branches of the oak on a display flight, clapping his wings under
and above his body as he goes, to descend on parachuting wings of bronze
displaying his black-and-white tail pattern.

The Bible contains several of the earliest references to bird migration,
and by far the nicest is to be found in the *Song of Solomon*:

> For lo, the winter is past, the rain is over and gone;
> The flowers appear on the earth; the time of the singing
>     of birds is come, and the voice of the turtle is
>         heard in our land.

The 'turtle' referred to is *not* the marine reptile (which is, in fact, more or
less voiceless) but the turtle dove, bronze-backed and a mixture of soft
fawns and pinks below.

Turtle doves are migrants, spending the winter months in Africa. They
build amazingly frail platform nests, sometimes on the outermost fringes
of the canopy of the oak but more often in a hawthorn bush nearby. The
nest is flat, and made of relatively few slender twigs: so few that the eggs
can usually be seen by looking up *through* the floor of the nest! How such
a skimpy structure survives the beefy youngsters – usually two in number
– is difficult to imagine, but it does, plus the added weight of the parent
birds when they visit bringing food. They eat a wide variety of seeds, but
fumitory is a special favourite, readily available all the time turtle doves are
in this country. Indeed, the maps of breeding distribution of the turtle dove
and of the occurrence of fumitory show a remarkable coincidence. Most
unusually in the bird world, the parent pigeons produce a sort of milk for
their young – popularly called 'pigeons' milk'. This is not strictly the same
as the milk of mammals, but is a highly nutritious secretion from the wall
of the pigeon's crop: white in colour, hence its name. On this rich diet, the
young grow rapidly.

Although they are among the latest migrants to arrive, and breeding is
usually not under way until mid- or late May, most turtle dove pairs attempt
to raise at least two broods, sometimes three, in their crowded stay in
Britain. At the end of August, and through September, flocks of these birds
will wing their way south, not only braving the natural hazards of long-
distance migration, but also running the lethal gauntlet of hunters in
southern Europe, where the turtle dove ranks high as a tasty delicacy.

For sheer song quality, the nightingale is generally regarded as the top avian songster. In the wood – as in many oakwoods in the southern and eastern parts of England – the nightingales are attracted each year to the dense scrub areas between the trees, occasionally in spring venturing up to the lower branches of the oak, there to pour forth their song. Heard as a solo at dead of night, this comes through the warm summer air as one of the most fabulous of songs, as near to perfection as is likely to be achieved. Part of the thrill of listening lies in the variety – from throaty chuckles to far-carrying whistles – and part in the total range, from rich cello-like phrases to the purest of treble fluting trills. For such superb songsters, nightingales are very drab in plumage, a case of 'not being able to have everything'. About halfway between robin and song thrush in size, they are chestnut-brown all over, enlivened only by a long, rich-rufous tail. This is often all that is seen, as generally nightingales are shy of coming into the open, preferring to scold intruders from concealment with a surprisingly varied repertoire of chacks and churrs.

For a bird so seldom seen, the nightingale is astonishingly well known to modern man. In the past, too, it was much appreciated, the ancient Greeks being fulsome in their praise of it. There are several traditional fables concerning the nightingale, one of which suggests that it sings with its breast against a thorn in order to keep awake. Oddly, the legendary reason for this wakefulness is that the nightingale, originally endowed with only one eye, stole the single eye that legend held the slow worm to possess. The slow worm is now on a vengeful hunt for the nightingale, which must sing all night to keep awake!

More modern references to this habit are legion, particularly among poets, for example Milton, in *Paradise Lost*:

> All but the watchful nightingale
> She all night her amorous descant sung.

This is not quite true, as nightingales sing a great deal during the daytime too, but their song tends to get swamped by the richness and variety of other bird song taking place in the wood at this time. However, *why* they sing so much at night is intriguing, and by no means well understood. Few songbirds sing after dark, but those that do tend to be birds of dense cover, like the nightingale. Also, and again like the nightingale, they are summer visitors to this country, migrating to and from wintering areas in Africa mostly at night. One theory has it that males migrate some days in advance of the females. On arrival, they set up territory and defend it by song, and then sing to the night skies to attract the females as they pass over. Although based on sensible logic, this leaves unexplained why they continue nocturnal singing until well into the breeding season.

*Nightingale*

The habit of singing – often loudly – long into the night does not find universal enthusiasm among those who live in nightingale country. An old Grecian poet urged the bird, 'Cease your din,' and Sir Alan Herbert, in *Temple*, says, 'I envy no man's nightingale.' Most, surely, would prefer to lie awake and listen, glorying in the song. As with so many birds with a rich folklore or fable tradition, there is a collective noun for a group of nightingales: a 'watch', derived from the same origins as the watch kept by sailors, sentries and nightwatchmen.

Following a rarely seen display which involves much ritualized posturing with wings drooped and fluttering and tail fanned, the nest is built low in the ground layer of vegetation or, quite commonly, on the ground. It is always well concealed from disturbance by humans or large predatory mammals or birds, though not safe from smaller predators like weasels or mice. The nest is usually made of dead leaves gathered from beneath the oak, with a skeleton framework of fine twigs or stout grass and a lining of fine grasses and hair. Because of its early departure on migration, the song period of the nightingale is short: song is unusual after June; and time normally allows the birds to produce just a single brood of speckled, young-robin-like fledglings.

In the shelter of the thick undergrowth around the oak, the nightingale (an inveterate skulker) behaves as a terrestrial thrush. Strong legs and large eyes are adaptations to this mode of life, as is the beak. Though not so stout as the conical beaks of the finches, nor so fine as that of insect eaters like the warblers, the 'half-way-house' beak of the nightingale allows it to tackle most soil and litter-dwelling invertebrate animals from tiny insects and spiders up to worms and caterpillars, and to turn to sugar-rich foods like berries as they become available later in the summer. At this time, the berries are invaluable in helping the bird to put on fat as a fuel reserve for the long migration south, which starts early, with birds deserting their breeding woods from late July onwards.

About this time of year there can be problems in the oaks with good songsters! One of the best ways of locating a territory-holding male is to hear him in song – indeed censuses to assess woodland bird populations can be based on this. But he must be correctly identified, and the main difficulty in the wood is that three of the best songsters – nightingale, garden warbler and blackcap – may each at some time use the oak as a song-post. All tend to be secretive, so it may not be easy to get a glimpse of the singing bird to see if it is the uniform russet-brown of the nightingale, the drab greenish-olive of the garden warbler or the greyish-bodied black-crowned blackcap. Thus it is obviously necessary to be able to identify the various songs without seeing the bird. Plenty of good records exist to allow practice before the season starts, but they, and the textbooks *and* the bird-song pundits forget one thing. Many birds love to mimic each other – indeed this may be how many of them learn to sing at least part of their repertoire. The wood has good numbers of nightingales, blackcaps and garden warblers – so they must all sing in close proximity to each other. Most birdwatchers acknowledge some slight difficulty with the last two – but, they say, it's easy when you get the hang of it. There is some aesthetic argument as to the order of merit in which the songs of blackcap and garden warbler should be put, but all agree that the nightingale is supreme. What can be found is that the nearer one species is to another species's territory, the more similar the two songs become, through extended song competitions and mimicry. So a solitary nightingale in a patch of hawthorn or blackthorn, surrounded by two or three blackcaps or garden warblers in the oaks, can influence these to such an extent that, although they may still easily be distinguished from the nightingale, they are difficult to separate from one another – it could be said that nightingale tuition had improved each beyond recognition.

Though their songs may be similar, subtle habitat preferences have evolved that enable the blackcap and garden warbler, two birds much the same size, and with much the same food needs, to partition their habitat to minimize harmful conflict. Though requiring some undergrowth for feeding and nesting, blackcaps favour the tall oaks and their extensive canopies for feeding and singing, while the garden warblers prefer those parts of the wood with fewer mature trees and denser undergrowth.

The sessile oakwoods of the wetter west and north of Britain hold two migrants, scarce even as visiting migrants in the south and east. One is the extremely handsome redstart, orange-breasted, red-tailed (*staert* is the Anglo-Saxon word for tail) and grey-backed, particularly striking during display when the male flits about among the tree trunks. Equally stunning is his choice of exposed song-posts to produce a briefly melodious jingle of song: these are often dead oak twigs, lit by a shaft of sunlight piercing the canopy and showing off his colours to the full. The other bird, though less colourful, is still smartly plumaged – the black-and-white pied flycatcher. Like the redstart, this is a hole-nesting bird, and it may be that one reason for its otherwise difficult-to-explain western preference is that oakwoods there are rarely intensively managed. On the lower, flatter lands of the east and south, commercial pressures now extending over centuries have led to 'hygienic' oakwood management, with regular removal of dead or dying timber and thus a limited supply of nest holes. In the west and north, the rugged terrain – with many oakwoods in steep-sided valleys and fewer commercial demands on poorer-quality timber – allows a more relaxed management and more decaying trees, and thus more nest sites.

The halcyon days of high summer may bring some unexpected sights in the wood. After many years of observations made regularly in one area, the feel of the place becomes instinctive and there develops a familiarity with its regular inhabitants and a sense of expectation for the surprises that it can occasionally spring. In common with other regularly watched woodland areas in southern England, rarely does a May or June pass without a golden oriole. In some areas in Britain these fabulous birds actually breed on occasion. As songsters they are as glorious as their rich golden-yellow and black plumage. Despite this apparently glaringly obvious colouration, put a male golden oriole in the dappled shade of the canopy of an oak, still with the yellow tinge of spring in its leaves, and he vanishes. The melodious, fluty whistling, with its characteristic 'chwee-loo-whee-oo' ending, continues, but sometimes an hour of eyestrain with the binoculars is necessary to obtain even the most fleeting glimpses of the bird itself. Interestingly, orioles are reasonably common quite far north on the Continent, and winter-visiting starlings to English gardens, arch-mimics that they are, may reproduce snatches of oriole song. This can be regarded as verbal confirmation of the ringing recoveries that indicate that many winter starlings come from the Baltic countries, including Poland, where orioles are numerous!

One of the more surprising birds, flighting during the early mornings and late afternoons over the open patches, is the shelduck. In living memory the wood, like others not far from sea or estuary, has not been without a few pairs of shelduck, nesting in 'burrows' constructed in the tangles of bracken and brambles. These handsome black and white, chestnut-girdled birds seem quite commonly to fall prey to the foxes, and all that is to be found of the nest is a scattering of the distinctive white down and a few eggshells. Those young that do hatch are shepherded by their parents soon after dawn on to the marsh, and they make their way by the small ditches and on foot out to the major fleets where they can be reared in safety. This extraordinary passage is put in the shade by the journeys (which make the photographic pages of local papers most years) undertaken by young ducklings on the way to the river, led by their parents over motorways or major trunk roads – some perishing on the former, but usually holding up the traffic on the latter.

On the marshland fringes of the oakwood, lining the boundary ditch, are some aged, part-hollow pollarded trees, and a quiet look at these is well worthwhile each June. One, in particular, is favoured by a female mallard each year – it can hardly be the same female as the tree has been used for decades – which builds a nest about 6 feet (2 m) up in the hollow crotch. If she is approached cautiously and absolutely silently she usually sits tight

*Mallard on tree nest*

and can be minutely inspected at 2-foot (60-cm) range. Occasionally, luck will allow an arrival more or less at the moment of hatching – giving time for a brief look at the rather bedraggled, still–damp ducklings before leaving quickly to let her marshal them in peace for the jump (at one day old!) down into the ditch.

More regular as August birds, all over the wood, are hawfinches, but their regularity detracts little from their fascination. Most years a few pairs breed – very discreet they are too, and most difficult to locate until the young are just about on the wing. Soon after fledging the family parties move out into the orchards to take advantage of first the cherries and later the plum crop – obviously not nowadays at a level likely to annoy the grower, although earlier this century this was the case in some parts. In August they return to the wood because the blackthorn fruit – the sloes – are ripe, and we see much more of them again. With binoculars, the full power of their massive beak – with an equally massive skull to which the necessary jaw muscles are attached – can be seen. The silvery beak is pyramidal, and about $\frac{3}{4}$ inch (18 mm) long, wide and deep. Some well-equipped research ornithologists have measured the pressure that the bill can exert at over 180 lbs per square inch! Such huge force is obviously needed to break open cherry and damson stones to reach the highly nutritious kernel within, and the hawfinches' other main food, the seeds of the hornbeam tree, are also very tough to open.

The woodcock is so unlike the rest of the wader family in habits and habitat that it holds a special fascination for many birdwatchers. For a start, its preferred habitat is woodland or forest, winter and summer alike, not the marshes or the mudflats. Most favoured are oakwoods like this one, with a deep layer of leaf litter, and with some areas of dry ground suitable for nesting and some expanses of damp soil for feeding. These wet areas, rich in the worms which are the major items in the woodcock's diet, are usually kept perpetually moist by seepage from underground springs. Besides this mixture of wet and dry ground, woodcocks also require a broken canopy and open glades or rides for their display flights.

Both in winter and in the breeding season, the woodcock is widespread in Britain and Ireland – more so than most birdwatchers would imagine, as its secretive habits often keep it from view. Because of its excellent camouflage the woodcock may be difficult to spot, but once seen it is very distinctive. It shares with the snipe a delicately streaked and mottled rich-brown plumage, absolutely ideal for concealment against a background of dead leaves or bracken. Most often, whether on the nest or feeding, the woodcock will rely on this amazingly good camouflage and crouch down, unmoving, until danger is within a few feet (or even inches)! It has, too, a disproportionately large beak like the snipe, about 3 inches (7.5 cm) long. It is a crepuscular bird, feeding and flying in the poor light of late evening, and so has evolved large eyes for better night vision which make the head seem large and angular. The pale bars on the head run cross-wise, unlike those of the snipe which run fore-and-aft. Compared with the snipe, which is very swift and nimble in flight, zig-zagging rapidly away over the marshes, the woodcock has a much heavier appearance. As it flies off between the trees it is so plump-bodied and round-winged that it could almost be mistaken for an owl.

About the only time that woodcock make themselves conspicuous in the oakwood is during their display flights. These usually take place at dawn or dusk, and are called 'roding'. Usually one and sometimes two or three birds will patrol a lengthy but regular circuit along the rides and across the open glades of the wood, using the oak as a turning point. The speed of flight is disconcerting, as the wingbeats seem very slow and again owl-like. As they fly, woodcock give a triple croak (a most unbird-like sound, quite reminiscent of a frog) followed immediately by a whistling 'tsiwick', like a bat. Round and round their beat the birds will go, sometimes for many minutes. Roding seems to be the only occasion when woodcock are at all gregarious (and gatherings of more than three birds are unusual): for much of the year they are the most solitary of the waders. Roding activity near the oak may start early in March, and often continues into June or July.

The nest is on the woodland floor, usually where there is plenty of leaf litter and often close to the bole of the oak where old leaves have gathered in a drift. 'Nest' is a rather grand term for it, as most often it is no more than a hollow scraped in the ground or leaves, with a lining of leaves. The typical clutch size – as in so many waders – is four, occasionally fewer or more. The ground colour of the eggs is off-white to buff, with a variable intensity of brown and rufous spotting and smudging rendering them near-invisible against the woodland floor. The female alone seems to carry the burden of incubating them for three weeks. Once they have hatched, the chicks' eyes are quickly open and in a few hours their camouflage-patterned down is dry enough for them to leave the nest. Although initially short-beaked, they fend for themselves under the watchful eyes of their parents, running about on sturdy legs. The beak grows rapidly, and so precocious are the young that they may be able to fly at fifteen to twenty days old, some time before they are fully grown.

Both adults and young probe in the soft soil for earthworms and insect larvae like leatherjackets: the rather swollen tip to the beak contains numerous sensitive nerve endings which allow the woodcock to identify its prey. Feeding at such a depth (down to 3 inches (7.5 cm)) would seem to present difficulties if a mouthful of mud is to be avoided with each worm. The woodcock manages this by means of a special skull adaptation. The nasal bones (which support the upper part of the beak) are long and flexible, and not rigidly attached to the roof of the skull between the eyes. Special muscles can pull these bones back, allowing just the tip of the beak to open and the worm to be grasped and eaten.

From time to time over many years, birdwatchers all over Britain and Ireland have reported seeing woodcock in flight carrying a youngster between their legs. A special enquiry into the status of the woodcock, conducted by the British Trust for Ornithology, received over 150 such sightings, and obviously the observers concerned felt quite certain about what they had seen.

*Woodcock*

Whether woodcock carry their young or not has been a topic for debate among ornithologists for over a century. Like all waders, the young leave the nest shortly after hatching and may wander about over a considerable area in company with their parents. The argument is that to move them this distance the parent birds sometimes clasp the chicks between their legs, holding them in place with a depressed tail and perhaps also with the long beak.

Sceptics point out that the woodcock (again, like many other waders) has a distraction display flight, designed to draw the attention of potential predators away from the young. This flight is laboured and clumsy, the tail is held depressed and the beak droops almost to the dangling legs. It usually ends almost in a crash-landing in the undergrowth, just as if the woodcock had been carrying a heavy burden.

With so many sightings on record, it becomes difficult to doubt the authenticity of them all, and most birdwatchers accept that carrying young is a regular, if rare, event. However, there is no photographic record, cine or still. The sceptics argue that, despite its secretive habits, the woodcock is a relatively well-studied and often-photographed bird, and surely some photographic confirmation should have been obtained by now. It seems that for certain people this problem will remain unresolved until such proof is obtained.

But the enigma of the woodcock does not finish here. From studies of its habitat, feeding habits and migratory patterns, zoologists have suggested that it, among other birds, may have played an important role in the distribution of certain microscopic soil animals. Their particular concern was to solve the age-old puzzle of how these small animals, like nematodes (often called eelworms, and ranging in length from 0.01–0.4 inches (0.5–10 mm)), recolonized much of Britain after the end of the last Ice Age, some 8000 years ago. Clearly the long period of permanently frozen soil would have eliminated all life. Subsequently, vegetation would have returned by the normal process of seed dispersal, and larger animals and birds would have moved in northwards, from their retreat around the Mediterranean, under their own steam. Some eelworms with resistant 'resting stages' might have blown in, and others parasitic in the seeds may have spread with plants. But zoologists have been particularly foxed by one group of eelworms which originate in damp oak woodland and which are agriculturally important because they spread virus diseases in crops. These eelworms lack a resting stage, feeding exclusively on plant roots in the soil.

There is evidence that, wriggling unaided through heavy soils like those in the wood, these eelworms might travel at best less than 3 feet (1 m) a year – or about 5 miles (8 km) since the end of the Ice Ages – certainly not enough to explain their widespread distribution in Britain's oakwoods. Nor were they transported by man on the roots of his crops, as they occur in greatest numbers in primeval woodland. In the search for an explanation, in terms of a means of transport, for such an eelworm to recolonize over such distances, the woodcock was considered to be one of the most likely carriers. The eelworms could survive for hours, perhaps days, in most soil on the beaks or feet of birds. Migrant woodcock, moving from one moist oakwood feeding area to another, and quickly feeding on arrival, could transport eelworms rapidly over hundreds of kilometres, introducing them to new areas. The woodcock migration pathway from Iberia, through France and then northwards throughout Britain, would seem ideal for the journey that the eelworms had to accomplish, and once they had become established in British woods, local woodcock movements and feeding could soon help them to become as widespread (in typical 'woodcock woods') as we now know them to be. Then, when farmers in centuries past felled the oakwoods to create fields, the eelworms turned their attention to man's crops as a source of food.

The summer months, too, are the best times to see those rather larger invertebrates, slugs and snails, around the oak. Though always spoken of as two separate types of animal, the slugs and snails really form just one group. The most obvious and striking difference to our eyes, that snails possess a shell, is just one of degree, because slugs are merely snails with a much-reduced or sometimes completely-missing shell.

Slugs and snails are typical of woodlands established on alkaline soils – the more chalky the soil, in general terms, the more numerous the slugs and especially snails, which use a great deal of the chalk's calcium when constructing their shells. Most, too, typically feed on the various mosses, fungi, grasses and wildflowers of the woodland floor beneath the oaks, though they can be a real hazard to the treelet oaks freshly sprouting from an acorn. Travelling on a ribbon of lubricating slime exuded from their extended foot, slugs and snails can cover considerable distances cross-country, and many are capable climbers. They eat by rasping away at leaves with their radula – for all the world like a miniature file – but some, like the glass snails, are carnivorous. Often these will use their radula and digestive juices to bore holes through the shells of other snails to feed (sometimes even as cannibals on their own species) on the soft body contents within. Other carnivorous snails and some of the testacellid slugs prey on worms. These they seize by extruding their mouthparts, slowly dragging the

*Slug eating oak seedling*

hapless worm from its burrow and consuming it. The testacellids carry a rather larger-than-usual relic of their shells on their back near the tail, and lying still in the soil seem at first glance to be quite inanimate, looking for all the world like a small piece of vermicelli spotted with a few traces of tomato ketchup.

These woodland molluscs are themselves not without their predators, however. Large stones on the paths through the oakwood are often used by song thrushes as anvils. Here the thrushes – the only birds in Britain really to exploit land snails as a food source – smash open the shells of those they have found, by the simple expedient of dashing them against the rock. The fragments of snail shell around the various anvils give a good indication of what the song thrushes are catching, and (as the other side of the coin) of how effective is the snail's camouflage. Under the oak it is fascinating to watch, as the season progresses, how the proportions of various coloured snails changes. One common snail, with a conspicuously banded mint-humbug-like shell usually less than 1 inch (2.5 cm) across, is called *Cepea*. It comes in various shades from green through to golden-brown, all with dark-brown stripes. Early in the season, the thrushes seem to catch more brownish forms than green. The reverse is the case as summer progresses and the grass yellows: then the golden forms have the advantage in camouflage terms, and it is the greenish ones that predominate among the fragments beside the anvil.

The humidity and shelter provided by the oak and its neighbours makes a good habitat for a range of slugs and snails, some tiny, some huge. Perhaps the most conspicuous under the tree, and the one capable of causing the sharpest of indrawn breaths in those who dislike such slimy creatures, is the giant black slug. This is a deciduous woodland specialist, disliking all forms of disturbance. In old-established forests with little human access and few forestry operations, it can reach a gigantic 16 inches (40 cm), but 4 or 5 inches (10–12.5 cm) would be a prime length near the oak.

Because of their need to conserve moisture, most slugs (and indeed snails) tend to be active more often at night than during the day, save when the weather is wet. Slugs conceal themselves in damp crevices under leaf litter and fallen bark, or more usually beneath stones, to emerge as the temperature falls and humidity rises during the evening. This is the time to see the great grey slug, a relative of the giant black but much more tolerant of man, even coming into gardens. The great grey is a widespread slug, with a varied diet mostly composed of fungi – even those that are poisonous to man – and decaying plant material.

In general, slugs and snails are hermaphrodite – that is, each one possesses the reproductive organs of both sexes, though these may not necessarily be mature at the same time. The 'courtship' of the great grey slug is elaborate in the extreme for so supposedly 'low' a creature. Often for an hour or more, two slugs will circle around each other, caressing with their tentacles. They will climb up to a broken-off rotten branch, sometimes at quite a height, and then lower themselves down, bodies elongated and entwined together, on a 'rope' of mucus. The slugs are often 2 or 3 inches (5–7.5 cm) long, or more, so this gives some idea of the amazing properties of the mucus. They remain entwined while a package of sperm passes from each to the other, gently spinning back and forth on their mucus suspension. Once mating is over, they separate, and one climbs back up the mucus. The other either drops off to the ground, or may eat its way back up the rope and on to the oak. Later on, their pearl-like eggs will be laid a few inches down in the soil.

The relative absence of bird song in the wood in July underlines the fact that high summer is here. So far as most of the oakwood birds are concerned, the business of territory-claim staking, attracting and keeping a mate demands song of the best quality produced at the greatest frequency and, with some exceptions, they have now achieved what there is to be achieved. Most young are on the wing, many by now quite independent of their parents and perhaps unlikely to come in contact with them ever again. Both the reduced volume and the leisured quality of the song confirm this suspicion that, for a while at least, the hard work is over. Temperatures on a fine day, with any breeze eliminated by the trees, soar high, and after noon the wood may be nearly silent.

Periods of quiet observation – preferably in the shade, back resting against the trunk of the oak – are called for, and after some minutes of stillness and silence (very precious commodities for the naturalist) the senses begin to take in more of what is going on. Rustlings in the long grass reveal themselves briefly, and tantalizingly, as shrews (probably pygmy shrews here), bank voles or long-tailed fieldmice. The last two are distinguished by their colour (the bank vole being a pleasantly rich chestnut brown), by the round head of the vole, and by the large ears and long tail of the fieldmouse. Down towards the fringes of the marsh it would be very surprising on a hot day not to see several grass snakes – possibly even one or two quite large ones, perhaps 3 feet (1 m) long and thumb-thick – and many lizards scampering around in the shorter, rabbit-cropped grass.

Everywhere birds *are* moving, feeding quietly under cover. Most are still in the drab juvenile plumage, although here and there a 'teenager' is visible – a young robin, for example, with blood-red patches on its breast beginning to replace the drab brown spots. Even allowing for the obvious fact that so soon after the breeding season youngsters are bound to outnumber their parents very considerably, the number of adult birds to be seen is still surprisingly low.

One reason for this may be that the business of moult, and keeping up the food intake that this energy-sapping business demands, is well under way. Equally, if the adults are in heavy moult, their powers of flight may be reduced – very much so, in some cases – and they will tend to keep to the safety of thick cover. Feathers are one of the strikingly distinctive features of birds – essential for flight and warmth – and serving a multitude of other vital functions, such as display to attract a mate. Made largely of the protein keratin, feathers must wear out. For example, some female blue tits have wings about $\frac{1}{4}$ inch (5 mm) shorter (on the standard $2\frac{3}{8}$–$2\frac{1}{2}$ inches (60–63 mm)) at the end of the breeding season than at the start. Naturally, nesting in holes and the frequent visits, first with nesting material, then with food, wriggling through a tight fit each time, contribute to an unusually high rate of wear, but in all small birds, a year is as much as can be asked of a feather before the need for replacement arises.

These feathers are secreted by special cells in the surface layers of the bird's body, and regrowth must take time and, of course, use up chemical energy. Not only is the study of moult fascinating biologically, but it assumes considerable importance as one of the major periods of stress during the bird's year. The blue tits and great tits, using the oak year-round, start moulting at the time (or sometimes before) the young leave the nest, in early June. From then on, moult proceeds at a leisurely pace. Rarely is more than one flight feather completely absent from each wing, although others will be in various stages of growth, so the 'missing' flight-feather area is unlikely to exceed twenty per cent of the total. Thus it would be surprising if the bird were ever severely inconvenienced, or endangered, although there are obviously slightly greater risks – for example, of being caught by a predator. Food demands are not much increased by energy needs of this level, and when moult occupies nearly one third of the year, as in the tits, few problems are likely to arise. This relatively slow moult seems to be general for year-round resident species in the oakwood, but (as always in nature!) there are exceptions – and these are difficult to understand. Good examples are the dunnock and the linnet, which moult in fifty or sixty days (sometimes less) against the hundred or so days of the tits. Perhaps food requirements as yet unknown dictate such speed, or perhaps it is a throwback to times past when these birds migrated. Some British linnets do move down to southern France and to Spain, and on the Continent the dunnock is a regular migrant.

The problems for migrant birds are *very* different. Having raised one or two families, they must move south from the wood before the food supply begins to fail and the climate to change for the worse. Instances of the pressures involved are demonstrated by two warblers in the oakwood, the whitethroat and its less conspicuous relative, the lesser whitethroat. After raising their last broods in the clearings or in the scrub patches early in July, most will be on the move southwards towards Africa in the latter part of August. Thus the process that takes a similar-sized bird, the great tit, a hundred days has to be rushed through in about forty-five by these two whitethroats! On occasions whitethroats may have six of the ten flight feathers missing (and perhaps with only about twenty per cent or less of their usual flight capability – enough to cause wonder at how they manage to get far enough off the ground to fly!). Not unnaturally, when in such heavy moult these species skulk even more than usual – not only because of the difficulties they have in flying, but because they must eat prodigiously to supply the necessary energy for new feather production. The blackcap has an only slightly less rushed moult, but its close relative, the garden warbler, has gone about things another way in the course of evolution. Garden warblers moult extremely rarely in this country – usually they delay moult until they reach their wintering grounds in Africa.

Young birds face different problems: there is no need for them to change the wing feathers they have grown in the nest – they will hardly have had a chance to wear out. But, and it is a big but, when in the nest, and shortly after fledging, they need to be as inconspicuous as possible, relying on their cryptic camouflage to protect them from predators; hence the drab browns and greys, the streaks and the spots. Long before next spring, however, they will want to compete with their elders for territory and for mates, and for this they need all the paraphernalia of full plumage for display purposes. Thus they do need to moult their body feathers, and in July and August large numbers of the rather ragged, parti-coloured 'teenagers' like the robin are to be seen foraging in and around the oak, capitalizing on its continuing rich insect population.

*Bracken*

# Autumn

CCORDING to John Keats, autumn is the 'season of mists and mellow fruitfulness', and to a large degree this is true of autumn in the oakwood. Botanically the plants are, in their multiplicity of ways, not so much closing down for the year as preparing to survive the inhospitable rigours of winter. Over much of Britain these conditions are such that only the evergreen trees (mostly conifers, but including the holly) and a small minority of herbaceous plants or small shrubs (the ivy and butcher's broom are good examples in the oakwood) will retain their leaves throughout.

Survival over winter can be accomplished in a number of ways. For a mature deciduous tree like the oak, with a substantial root system, all that is necessary (on the face of it) is to shed the leaves, which are tender and vulnerable to frost and snow. The 'goodness' in terms of food that these leaves have produced during photosynthesis through the summer has been transferred through the oak's vascular system (akin, loosely speaking, to the veins and arteries of an animal) to the roots. Some has already been used to increase the size of the tree by means of new shoots, and some has gone to form the buds from which the next season's growth will come. These buds are well protected by tough bud-scales from the elements and are able to survive, dormant (as the sap has largely flowed back to the roots), until the warmer weather of returning spring starts the sap flow and rekindles active life. The outward sign in autumn that this is taking place is the shedding of the leaves. At summer's end, the vessels transporting sap to and from the leaves gradually close, and the leaf yellows and falls. The timing of leaf fall can vary very considerably from year to year on the oak – perhaps by as much as a month – and the same is true for its neighbours in the wood, so every year the golden spectacle of autumn colour is an extended display.

At the other end of the size scale in the wood are those annual plants growing in the shadow of the oak, plants like the various willowherbs, cleavers (or goose-grass), scarlet pimpernel and narrow-leaved vetch, which perish with the first serious frosts of the autumn and rely on seed produced and dispersed earlier in the year for their reappearance next spring. Others, though in the same size category, are longer-lived, like the yellow pimpernel (perhaps even more widely appearing in the oakwood than its scarlet cousin) and several others of the vetch (or pea) family. In these, frosts greatly reduce the above-ground parts of the plants – they may even vanish to all intents and purposes – but the underground parts survive. Usually these underground parts are in the form of a tap root (like a miniature parsnip) or rhizomes, which are in essence underground stems; the wood anemone is a case in point. Another underground system is the bulb, best seen in the oakwood where badgers or foxes have been digging and exposed the soil beneath the bluebells that were so prominent in spring.

These organs are capable of holding stored foods in the shape of starch or sugars, and are protected from the cold both by the layer of soil above them and by the 'anti-freeze' properties of sugar-rich, highly concentrated sap. Of course, it is not just the annual plants that produce seeds: though for the annuals it is vital that seed is set and dispersed every year, almost all the perennials from the lowly pimpernel to the majestic oak itself attempt to set some fruit annually.

So what is the range of this 'mellow fruitfulness' so far as the various plants are concerned, and what is its value to the other inhabitants of the oakwood? Autumn is the time of setting of seed – where both the ripening process and the quantity of seed produced reflect in various ways the quality of the weather of the preceding summer. Heavy rainful or drought, too low or too high temperatures at the wrong time can each influence the quantity and quality of seed produced, as can the impact of diseases like mildew and insects (in agricultural circumstances they would be called 'pests') ranging from aphids to weevils and wasps.

How this seed is dispersed provides a fascinating array of structural adaptations. Dispersal away from the immediate vicinity of the parent plants is almost invariably a good thing, and wider dispersal is clearly potentially of benefit to the plant species as a whole. Most of us are familiar with some of these seed adaptations to dispersal, if only because we have had to disentangle seeds from our clothing. One of the best examples must be the aptly named cleavers, recognizable by the clinging nature of its stems and leaves but also distinguished by its clambering habit, ridged stem and whorls of assegai-shaped leaves, each ring positioned at intervals up the stem and a couple of inches in diameter. The 'adhesive' properties come from a multitude of tiny hooks on the stem and leaf surfaces, and the round seed, about half the size of a pea, is similarly adorned, though its hooks are rather more robust. The purpose of such an adaptation is clear – such seeds would cling to the coat of any passing animals and be transported for varying distances before being brushed off on vegetation or groomed out by the animal itself, the aim being that they should germinate where they fall. Many of the grass seeds are protected by spiked and bristly projections from being eaten by birds or small rodents, but these protective awns are often themselves covered in minute hooks and, like those of cleavers, these seeds also get tangled in the fur of passing animals.

Beneath the oak, on the bare patches of soil that seem to occur in most summers, the two pimpernels flourish. Both tend to drop their seeds nearby, with no adaptation for wider dispersal. Even so, the passing feet of animals, especially rabbits, and physical disturbance of the surface soil by either heavy rainfall or the action of leaves blown by a strong wind, achieve a modicum of spread.

Two other small plants favour these bald patches, both members of the willowherb family. The scarce willowherb is found in the damper areas of the wood, to be replaced by the rather larger and deeper-pink-flowered, spear-leaved willowherb on dry patches. Usually between 6 inches (15 cm) and a couple of feet tall, these willowherbs carry each of their four-petalled flowers (about $\frac{1}{4}$ inch (6 mm) across) at the top of a long seed-capsule – often 2 inches (5 cm) or more in length. The capsules open when ripe to reveal tiny dark spherical seeds,

*Blowing thistledown*

each with a long feathery tail – called a chalazal plume. The purpose of this plume is the same throughout the family, but is best and most dramatically demonstrated in the rose-bay willowherb, or fireweed, a foxglove-sized plant usually occurring in great masses on recently disturbed soil or where fire has eliminated the previous vegetation. Once the seed-pods have split open, the wind takes hold of the plumes and blows the seeds often for very considerable distances, perhaps even miles. The same principle is used by dandelions, their spherical 'clocks' blown apart by the wind throughout the summer, and by various thistles in the woodland clearings, though 'thistledown', the seed being rather larger and heavier, does not have the flight range of willowherb seeds.

Yet other fruits have been shaped by evolution to involve birds as their agent for dispersal. It is no accident that the fruits of blackberry, rose, hawthorn and elder are strikingly coloured, borne in conspicuous clusters, and rich in sugars and thus good food value. The actual seeds of these shrubs are concealed within a coating of desirable flesh: they are the 'pips' familiar to us as blackberry eaters. Hard and woody, these pips pass through the digestive tract of birds undamaged, but by the time they are excreted again, the bird that ate the fruit may have flown a considerable distance, which is highly effective dispersal.

For some of the birds of the oakwood, it could be said that the start of autumn is heralded by the fruiting of most of the plants that carry berries, both in the clearings and within the trees. Primarily this involves the blackberry and the elder – and, as any gardener knows, the birds often do not bother to wait for the fruit to ripen before eating it. For many species, like the warblers, about to migrate southwards, this sugar-rich fruit is absolutely vital. It needs little searching out, can be eaten quickly, and is obtainable in prodigious quantities with little effort. What is most difficult for us to understand is how a bird like a whitethroat or a blackcap, having fed for so many months almost entirely on insects, and having raised its young on the same food, can suddenly change from this difficult-to-digest protein-rich diet to one so completely vegetarian.

It seems most probable that this dietary change occurs not long after the last brood of young have fledged, at the start of the relatively rapid period of moult. If this is the case, then doubtless the high-energy food helps cope also with the strain of the moult. But there is another very significant purpose. Stored fatty materials, or lipids, serve as an insulating layer and as an overnight energy store for our resident birds, especially during the cold winter weather. For the migrants, similar fat stores serve as fuel, to be used up steadily *en route*. The greater the quantity of stored fat, the greater the non-stop range of the migrant.

*Blackcap*

Recent studies of bird weights, both in the USA and in Britain, continue to reveal astonishing aspects of bird migration. How birds navigate remains perhaps one of the greatest unsolved mysteries in biology: now we know that not only do they get there accurately, but some reach Africa in one hop, and it is conceivable that others can even over-fly the Sahara from southern England. Probably the best illustrative examples are wetland birds, the reed and sedge warblers. The former increase in weight by only about thirty per cent in autumn, and ringing recoveries show that they first make landfall, after leaving this country, in southern France and the Iberian peninsula – just about the distance the energetics experts tell us they should be able to achieve. Here they rest and feed furiously, perhaps for several days, laying down sufficient reserves for the next stage of their journey south. Sedge warblers, on the other hand, increase in weight by one hundred per cent or more – there are layers of fat everywhere so that the birds are nearly spherical and certainly have to struggle to get airborne – and there are almost no ringing recoveries between here and their winter quarters in Africa, probably mostly south of the Sahara! This indicates that the journey may often be a non-stop one, however difficult this is to comprehend.

Quite clearly, from the purple colour of the droppings they produce, many birds rely on the blackberries and elderberries growing in the more open areas of the wood for autumn food. This applies to both residents and migrants, to those birds which, like the thrushes, are considered as 'omnivores', eating both fruit and small animals, and to others (like the summer migrants, the warblers and the nightingale) which may tend to be regarded, loosely, as insectivorous. A study of autumn weights is revealing: looking at just two of the birds that have spent many hours of the summer singing in the oak, the robin and the blackcap, there are considerable differences. Obviously one is a regular migrant, the other not. The robin has a midsummer weight – its leanest period stretching from April to August – of around 20 grams, which rises through the autumn to a winter peak of around 22 grams, a ten per cent increase. For comparison, similar figures for the dunnock would be a summer weight of 22 grams and a winter weight of 24 to 25 grams, again a ten per cent rise. The blackcap, arriving with its 'fuel supplies' almost exhausted in April at about 15 grams, soon reaches a summer weight of 16 or 17 grams; but during the autumn, gorging as fast as it can, it puts on weight speedily. Many will depart these shores weighing 22 grams (a fifty per cent increase on arrival weight) and some as much as 26 grams, a phenomenal seventy-five per cent increase achieved in a couple of months.

Perhaps it is just as well that autumn is such a fruitful period and that an abundance of food remains, for October sees the start of an inward rush of birds to replace those summer migrants off and away south. A glance at a weather map of the northern hemisphere in any atlas will give some clues as to why. Look at the pattern of the isotherms – the lines joining places of equal temperature at a given time of year. Most often, the two given are for January and July – both mid-season for the birdwatcher. Some detailed studies have been carried out over Europe to discover how bird movements are related to temperatures, the classical example being the northward movement of swallows in spring. Birdwatchers all over Britain and the Continent, spanning north-south as well as east-west, recorded the date of the arrival of their first swallow in spring, and the 'front' – the vanguard of the hordes of these birds moving north – was found to be almost precisely the same shape, and to move at the same speed, as the 10°C isotherm.

This illustrates how close the association between weather and birds can be; and a look at the January (midwinter) picture will confirm the fact. Imagine the isotherms appearing much the same as altitude contour lines on a map. In central and eastern Siberia, there is a centre of extremely low temperature, with January averages way below *minus* 30°C. The January isotherms do not follow the parallels of latitude so that, latitude for latitude, the oceanic coast of western Europe is very much warmer: London may be up to 30°C warmer than Lake Baikal on the same latitude in Russia. For migratory birds wishing to take advantage of the summer climate and food supply in the vast areas of northern Europe and Asia, a considerable barrier exists to the simple north-south migration that might seem obvious: it is the belt of mountains from the Himalayas right across to the Alps north of the Mediterranean. While these mountain ranges are not totally impassable, they have lent their weight to the development of a marked south-westerly trend in many bird migration routes originating in central Eurasia and eastern Europe. Birds move away from climatic conditions which make it impossible for the majority to survive (there are, naturally, specialist exceptions like our ptarmigan that can continue despite the snows because of adaptations in both structure and way of life) and for many the most practicable route – defined by millennia of evolutionary failures and successes – has become the south-westward one to Britain and Ireland.

Thus the west coast of Europe, including Britain, should expect perhaps even an increase in the total number of birds that the countryside supports when winter comes.

An additional factor may also influence the number of some of our winter visitors. A series of good breeding seasons and mild winters, with an abundant food supply, may allow their numbers to build up to such an extent that their sheer weight imposes impossible strains on the available food, and perhaps also on the social organization of the species concerned. The best-known example of this phenomenon in animals is the approximately four-year cycle in lemming numbers. When the population of these attractive little rodents – widespread in northern Continental Europe – reaches its peak size, westward mass emigration begins in search of pastures new. Often the size of the migration, the obviously abnormal mental state of the lemmings and the hordes that perish in fruitless attempts to cross the Atlantic Ocean makes newspaper headlines.

It seems likely that much the same reason lies behind the periodic arrival in Britain of some most attractive birds – the so called 'irruptive' species, the crossbill, which visits conifer woodland, the waxwing and (less commonly) the nutcracker, both of which may be seen in the oakwood on rare occasions. Because these species are so rarely seen, the possibility is often overlooked that other species which are commonly seen may behave in the same way. The tits are a good example. In much of northern Europe the needs must be migratory anyway, and when numbers are built up by a long period of good conditions, an absolute avalanche of birds may descend on to Britain. The last time this happened, in 1957, there were not only extraordinary numbers, but some extraordinary behaviour too. No milk bottle was safe, and there were many complaints in letters to the newspapers about tits entering houses and tearing off strips of wallpaper! In the absence in recent years of a really severe winter, it seems fair to predict that the time is becoming ripe for a repetition of this spectacle.

In most years, looking at the oak or walking through the wood in October, it is difficult not to be conscious of just how many tits there are. Some of the already large summer groups have coalesced into huge flocks, sometimes a hundred birds or more strong. It is easy to visualize the pressures building up on birds now – food supplies in some cases are diminishing and alternative sources must be found, in competition with the more experienced adult birds that have faced the problems before. Research at Oxford University has suggested that by November most of the young which are going to succumb will have done so. This may not be precisely the case all over Britain, but before next spring, die most of them must – a brutally matter-of-fact statement, perhaps, but no old adage is truer than that which describes nature as 'red in tooth and claw'. Tit mortality rates were discussed in the summer chapter, but can in autumn be viewed in a different way. With no mortality operating and breeding at a normal rate, one pair of blue tits will have given rise to more than 2000 individuals after five years. Unless the population of blue tits is to escalate frighteningly, a threat to its own food resources and those of other species, the high mortalities suggested earlier (fifty per cent for adults; ninety per cent for young) must operate. Is all this death necessary, though? Evolutionarily speaking, the answer must be yes, because in this way the population retains sufficient elasticity to exploit environmental changes or to cope with adversities like severe winters or epidemic disease: if the clutch size were to be tailored too precisely, there would be no leeway, insufficient flexibility in the system to allow the situation to be quickly remedied.

While this sort of calculation about mortality can be made with relative ease, it is much more difficult to assess how the recovery phase works. The last really extended severe winter, back in 1962–3, had a dramatically adverse effect on woodland birds, with population reductions in various species ranging from twenty to eighty per cent. Censuses showed that, in many areas, numbers of most species were 'back to normal' three or four years later, though some (green woodpecker and barn owl, for example) recovered much more slowly. Yet an analysis of the breeding results in the 1963 and 1964 summers showed no real evidence of the increase in clutch size that many people expected. Despite this, the populations recovered. In some way, presumably, the mortality rate had been reduced, allowing numbers to increase again. Obviously it is ridiculous to suggest that cats had declared a truce with blackbirds and song thrushes, or that car drivers were taking extra care as they knew that numbers were low. The explanation of this process is still being sought, and until the reason is found, biologists and birdwatchers together will be able to delight in arguing about this apparent evidence that mortality rates are influenced favourably by low population density.

Anthropomorphically speaking, if some plants seem to set out to attract birds, with the goal of getting their seeds dispersed, others seem to regard birds as major predators on their seed stocks and to go to some lengths to protect them. Clearly the finch family must be seen as the biggest potential threat, as all their beak and digestive tract adaptations are towards a seed-eating way of life. The phenomenal crushing power of the hawfinch beak has already been mentioned, but the diet of this bird is relatively restricted. Of more general danger to most plants are species like the linnet, relatively uncommon among the oaks as it is a hedgerow and scrub bird, or its smaller, darker relative the redpoll. Not much larger than a tit, and almost as agile, the redpoll gets its name from a deep crimson patch on top of its head (or poll). In the oakwood its song, a high-pitched purring trill, is a noticeable summer feature, but as it is produced in a circling flight high in the sky and as it is such a small bird, it cannot itself be called conspicuous.

In autumn the redpoll's plumage is drabber and it spends much time on the ground, seeking out the huge range of small seeds. Seeds, by their very nature, are a good food supply, containing the 'concentrated goodness' on which the emerging plantlet is going to grow. Thus they are popular as a food source, not just with birds but also with beetles, mice and voles. This concentrated level of predation, which will persist (on the steadily diminishing stock of seed) through the autumn and the winter, is one reason why seed production seems to human eyes vastly in excess of requirements, because sufficient must remain undiscovered and uneaten to provide next spring's plants.

One plant that grows in the open spaces near the oak seems specially well protected against bird attack. From the birds' point of view, if they can eat the ripening seeds on the plant (as a bullfinch does ashkeys), their food source is compact and feeding not very time-consuming, an important factor as the short days of winter approach. The thistle family, some of them now of a considerable size, and the teazel, with its spiky clusters of blossoms (and later seeds) protected by long, needle-sharp spines, are well defended against most finches – but not the goldfinch. Although still basically conical, or wedge-shaped, like the beaks of other finches, the goldfinch beak has tips elongated into fine points, almost like a pair of tweezers, to enable it to extract seeds from these inhospitable surroundings.

The goldfinch is very much the harlequin of the bird world with its black cap, red and white face, pale buff belly and black wings with the broadest bar of pure gold feathers. Perhaps it is seen at its best on the thistle-heads of autumn, with its colours set off against green leaves and purple flowers. As it moves from seed-head to seed-head, the continuous sparkling of colours gives a clue to the origins of the collective noun for a group of goldfinches – a 'charm'. The word could equally well apply to the song, typically with a few warming-up notes to clear the throat preceding an extended tinkling trill. Obviously a bird with such a variety of attractions to human eyes and ears runs the tragic risk of its beauty being its undoing. For the goldfinch this is indeed the case: in Britain until quite recently and even today on the Continent (in Belgium particularly) tens of thousands of these birds are trapped each year and caged. Despite the efforts of the Royal Society for the Protection of Birds, in Britain even now an illegal and unsavoury black-market bird-catching trade persists. Such activities are difficult to track down, and it is to be hoped that new legislation

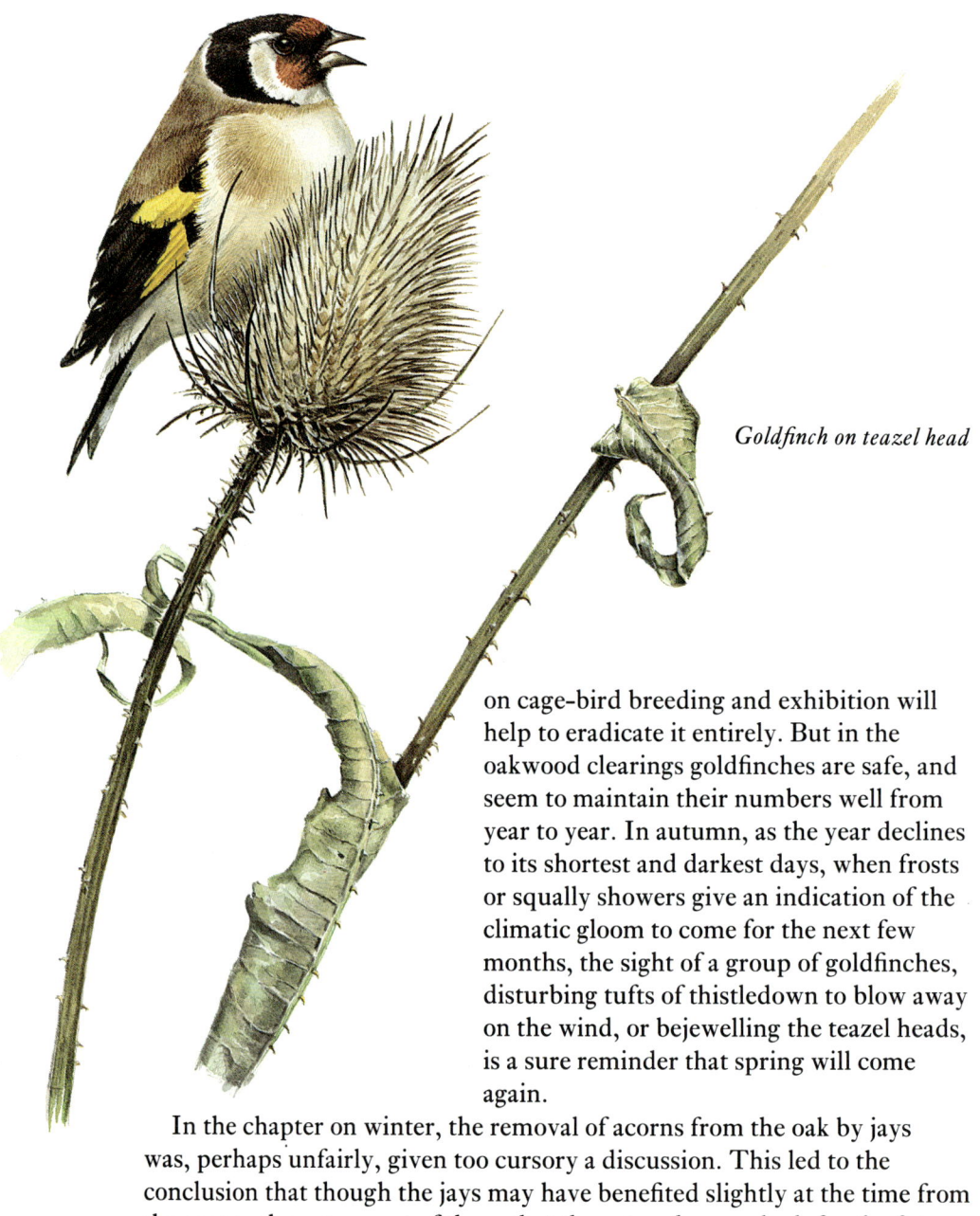

*Goldfinch on teazel head*

on cage-bird breeding and exhibition will help to eradicate it entirely. But in the oakwood clearings goldfinches are safe, and seem to maintain their numbers well from year to year. In autumn, as the year declines to its shortest and darkest days, when frosts or squally showers give an indication of the climatic gloom to come for the next few months, the sight of a group of goldfinches, disturbing tufts of thistledown to blow away on the wind, or bejewelling the teazel heads, is a sure reminder that spring will come again.

In the chapter on winter, the removal of acorns from the oak by jays was, perhaps unfairly, given too cursory a discussion. This led to the conclusion that though the jays may have benefited slightly at the time from the acorns they ate, most of those that they stored, or cached, for the future remained unfound and were more likely to give rise to further generations of oak trees! Students of the behaviour of members of the crow family would certainly disagree with this view. Many would argue that the case

*Acorn cluster*

of the oak and the jay is an example of an association between a plant and its seeds and a bird that is so closely knit it could almost be described as a symbiosis.

Jay experts would suggest that acorns are the main autumn and winter food supply, even indeed more than that, as many of the hidden acorns are fed on by the jays in spring. At this time they may help, as a nutritious food source, to 'build up' the birds for the oncoming breeding season, and in some years their use may persist through into the summer months, when they can be fed to the recently fledged young. Experts would also suggest that both experimental evidence and observations in the wild indicate that jays retrieve a high proportion of the acorns that they cache, being able to find them even beneath a layer of snow. As the acorns are without doubt the major overwintering food source for the majority of jays, it is impossible to argue against this evidence. So far as the oak is concerned, its life-span and acorn production is such that only a minute proportion of its acorns will give rise to other oaks, so the few that the jays remove and transport, and then cannot find again, will serve well enough the purposes of seed dispersal.

Like so many other biological events, acorn crops on the oak, and its neighbours, vary from tree to tree and from year to year. There may be years of local scarcity, and in these (so effective is their crop-discovery system) all the jays of the area converge on those woods, or trees, that are carrying a worthwhile supply. These are the times when jays can be seen singly or in groups, flopping over open countryside towards the best feeding, returning after each foray to their home wood. Sometimes such movements are so conspicuous that they give rise to the mistaken impression that a migration is occurring, for jays, especially in years of acorn-crop failure on the Continent, do occasionally appear in sizeable flocks in autumn.

The neatness and practicality of this symbiosis between jay and oak is seen at its best in autumn. Jays from all over the wood visit our oak, plucking the ripening acorns with no difficulty and flying off, usually with two or three in their crop and one held crosswise in the beak. Should the

acorn crop have failed, the jays
must turn to such similar foods
as they can find. The most obvious
of these is the sweet chestnut, but
watching a jay tackle the very
prickly seed-coat gives the
impression that this is a
difficult and time-consuming
task, added to which the bird
usually seems to depart with only a
single 'nut' to show for its pains – nowhere
near so efficient as acorn eating.

*Jay*

Occasional failures of the crop are a feature of
all plants, as any farmer or gardener knows, and from
time immemorial they have occurred on the oak. Most
recently – in fact very much in the last few years – in some areas
repeated wholesale acorn-crop failures have worried both those particularly
keen on jays *and* those (and this applies to just about everyone) concerned
about the future of the oak in the British countryside. Alarm over
impending disaster quickly achieves wide circulation in our media-
conscious world: just what is the problem, and how severe is it likely to
become?

The answers to these questions are quite fascinating, and the story has
too a touch of 'David and Goliath' about it, for the prime cause of this threat
to the mighty oak is a tiny wasp. Early in the 1960s, strange galls – for all
the world resembling miniature chocolate ice-creams of the soft 'whirl'
variety – were spotted on acorns in southern England. Over the next decade
or more, little attention was given to this oddity, save that that the creature
that caused the galls was identified as a French wasp called *Andricus quercus*
which was thought perhaps to have blown across the Channel. In recent
years, more of these strange knobbly galls have been found in many
southern counties, but matters came to a head in 1983, when vast numbers
of acorns (including many of those in our wood) were destroyed. The
shortfall in the acorn harvest was such that creatures as diverse as jays and
squirrels, woodmice and weevils had in many areas to find alternative foods.
For jays and squirrels – the largest and most obvious creatures affected –
there were increased records of garden visits, bread and fruit eating, and
flocks of jays were to be seen scouring the countryside for suitable
nourishment.

During this period the galls were given a name, knopper galls, and some
research has been carried out on the causative wasp. What happens, it

seems, is that the adults emerge from galled acorns in March and fly to a Turkey oak somewhere in the vicinity. There, without mating (strange, but typical of many pest insects), the females lay hundreds of eggs. From these, in June, emerges a second adult generation of wasps, which fly off in search of a pedunculate oak (the typical lowland oak) and lay their eggs, many fewer this time, in the tiny young acorns. As knopper gall wasp larva and acorn grow, the activities and secretions of the larva cause a cell response in the acorn that gives rise to the strange gall. In autumn these lightweight deformed acorns, of little or no value to the traditional acorn eaters, fall to the woodland floor, each containing hibernating wasp larvae which will emerge, to set the cycle going again, next spring.

The Turkey oak seems quite unaffected by its part in these proceedings, but acorn crops of the pedunculate oak have suffered excessively in many areas right across England. Conservationists are concerned not just that numbers of our traditional oak may be dramatically reduced, but also that the alien Turkey oak may take advantage of the lack of competition from native species and establish a supremacy from which it would be hard to dislodge. And there are the legion of creatures, large and small, dependent on the native pedunculate species to be considered: though indirect, the impact of this oak parasite could be for them just as damagingly dramatic.

But what of the situation in France, where oaks have had to endure the knopper gall wasp for centuries? French foresters are unconcerned by the problem, because 'biological control' deals with it. There, as it is an indigenous species, it has its own array of parasites and predators, and these combine to keep knopper gall wasp numbers at an acceptably low level. Thus far, none of these specific predators has achieved the Channel crossing, but the way is now open for some of our own gall wasp parasites to set about the foreign invader. Control with insecticides, which would be most unlikely to succeed, is an appalling thought because of all the other insects that would needlessly be slaughtered. Far, far preferable would be the introduction to this country of some of the predators and parasites so effective on the Continent. So the battle is by no means yet lost, and the future of our oak and its animal life far less threatened than some gloomy forecasts would have us believe.

Galls are no novelty to the oak. As with insect numbers, there are probably more different types of gall recorded on oaks than on any other plant. Many, too, have extraordinarily complicated life-cycles. Almost any insect, particularly one sucking out the sap, will cause some distortion of the host oak cells, but these odd bumps and swellings hardly merit the term gall. For practical purposes, it is better to consider a gall as something distinct. From the point of view of the causative insect, the specially

*Marble galls*

*Knopper gall*

developed tissue that it has caused the plant to form will offer both food and shelter. Strange as it may seem, there is a positive side from the oak's viewpoint too, in that the troublesome foreign 'invader' of its tissue is localized both in space and in impact once the gall is formed, cut off, as it were, from being able to cause more trouble.

One of the most obvious galls, both in our oak and on many others, especially scrub oaks in hedgerows, is the 'oak marble'. This is near-spherical, brown and woody-looking, $\frac{1}{2}$ to 1 inch (12–25 mm) in diameter, often with a neatly drilled, woodworm-like hole visible on one side where the gall wasp has emerged. It is not to be confused with the oak-apple gall, which is softer and irregular in shape. The history of the oak marble has some parallels with the knopper gall, and indeed it is caused by a wasp of the same genus, *Andricus kollari*. Believe it or not, this gall wasp was introduced deliberately into Britain, where it is now widespread. It was brought to Devonshire from the Levant – in the Middle East – in about 1830. The galls are very rich in tannic acid, and were at the time used in both the production of cloth dyes and ink manufacture. Like other gall formers, *Andricus kollari* undergoes a process called the alternation of generations. The oak marbles are caused by females of an asexual generation, and in this case the galls of the sexual generation are relatively scarce, occurring only on the Turkey oak (again) and to such a small extent that it is questioned if they are always involved. In some years it seems that the life-cycle runs from year to year in the asexual phase only on the native oaks, because few Turkey oaks may occur in substantial areas with high levels of infestation. It may be that the knopper gall behaves similarly.

The gall wasps as a group show little resemblance to the typical wasps that hover round the jam, even to the rather stunted specimens about in autumn. Few reach $\frac{1}{2}$ inch (12 mm) in length and few have a wingspan in excess of 1 inch (25 mm) at the very most. Their abdomen tends to be flattened from side to side, giving them more the appearance of a 'flying ant' (the winged sexual phases of the lawn ants, for example, that emerge on hot days during the summer). Mostly they are ginger or dark brown to black in colour, without the striking bands of black and yellow of the familiar wasp, and this if anything adds to their apparent resemblance to flying ants. In contrast to the ants, though, they have long, slender, whip-like antennae, while most ants have a distinct 'elbow joint' part way along their antennae.

The true oak apple, caused by *Biorhiza pallida*, is a much better example of the alternation of generations, a reproductive tactic designed to make the best of all circumstances. With two methods available, sexual and asexual (with and without the need for the meeting and mating of the sexes, and in many ways paralleled in plants by propagation from seed or from cuttings), the sexual phase usually follows a period of plentiful food and precedes one of scarcity. As a general rule, the sexual generation – males and females – develop rapidly in galls formed early in the year on catkins, buds or leaves, and these, after mating, are the parents of the asexual (or agamic) generation, which in the case of the oak-apple gall wasps, develops underground.

With such a cyclic life-history, it is difficult to know how to 'begin at the beginning', so let us start the story in early autumn. The fertilized female gall wasps of the sexual generation burrow into the soil in late summer to find oak rootlets into which they insert their eggs. The laying of the egg triggers off a response in the root cells that creates irregular brown underground galls about $\frac{1}{4}$ inch (6 mm) across, often to be found in clusters or coalescing into an apparently single larger gall. Within these galls the larvae mature for about fifteen months, so the emerging female (of the asexual generation) leaves at the end of the second winter. She emerges wingless, and clambers up trunks and stems to lay her eggs (through a robust and sharply pointed ovipositor) at the base of a leaf bud on a twig. This process almost severs bud from twig, and the ensuing gall develops rapidly through the spring. It is spongy in texture and irregularly spherical, 1 inch (25 mm) or more in diameter. By midsummer, the galls are conspicuous, and a pale pinkish-green in colour, perhaps the reason for naming 29 May, which commemorates the restoration of Charles II to the throne, as oak-apple day. It is unlikely that the name bears any relation to the other association of Charles II with this tree, for when he hid in the famous Boscobel oak after the Battle of Worcester, fought on 3 September, the galls would have withered away. Out of these galls emerge male and female sexual-generation adults, both sexes winged, and after mating, it is the female that sets off towards the oak roots.

The gall wasp does not have it all its own way, though. Within the bud galls particularly, and to a lesser extent the root galls, a complex situation can develop. First, other small wasps have hit on the 'energy-saving' tactic of inserting their eggs in the nutritious gall created by another species. These 'hitch-hikers' or 'unpaying guests' can hardly qualify as parasites and are called 'inquilines'. True parasites are there too, of course. Other wasps, again, seek out galls and, with extremely long and sharp ovipositors, position their egg with unerring accuracy within the developing larva, which is destroyed as the parasite grows. Amazingly enough, even the parasite-within-its-host-within-its gall is not safe, for hyperparasitic wasps occur which parasitize the developing parasite in its turn!

Probably the most familiar of the range of galls on the oak, countrywide too, in the autumn, are spangle galls. These reddish, flying-saucer-like spangles up to $\frac{1}{4}$ inch (6 mm) across are induced by gall wasps of a different genus, *Neuroterus*. At least four separate species may be involved, each causing rather different galls both in the autumn and in the spring. One feature is common to all of them, and that is the pattern of the life-cycle. The spangle develops its own abscission layer (the layer of special cells cutting off a leaf from the stem) early in the autumn and falls to the ground beneath the tree before the oak leaves themselves fall. In this way, when the leaves fall soon after, they provide an insulating layer against winter frosts and a concealing cover from the greedy eyes of birds anxious for a tasty morsel. In spring, a single female gall wasp emerges from each spangle and, without fertilization, lays her eggs in either bursting buds or young, just-expanding leaves. The most familiar spangle is reddish – this is the common spangle gall. Smaller, rather hairy and green in colour, with a more deeply cupped appearance, is the cupped spangle gall, while the smooth spangle gall is hairless

*Spangle galls*

and yellowish, and the silk-button spangle golden brown and covered in fine shiny hairs.

The sexual-phase gall wasps' homes also differ: the common variety induces currant galls, very like a truss of redcurrants, in the male catkins; the silk-button gives blister galls, about an $\frac{1}{8}$ inch (3 mm) across, in the leaf blade; the cupped a pea-sized (and -shaped) hairy gall (hairy pea gall) on the underside of a leaf vein; and the smooth a much smaller pea (Schenck's gall) on the leaf margin. So the various spangle gall wasps partition their ecological resources by choosing different sites for the galls of their sexual generations, but there must be considerable competition on the undersides of the leaf when the sexual generation female is ovipositing to set up the gall for the asexual phase. There is some indication that excess strife is 'avoided' by the wasps laying not only on different parts of the leaf (though these differences are poorly defined) but also on different regions of any given oak tree, with the silk-button near the top, the smooth nearer the bottom, the common in the middle and heart of the tree, and the cupped (which tends to be the latest to emerge) an opportunist that seeks out any vacancies still available.

So a closer inspection of this apparently simple range of 'warts' on the face of the oak reveals natural history at its most fascinating. The creatures that cause the galls show an intriguing alternation of generations, each generation causing quite a different gall. Each gall-former has its own problems to bear in the way of hyperparasites and inquilines, far from being safe and sound within its vegetable shelter as might be expected. Ecologically, in various ways they sort out when and where to attack the oak – partitioning of resources at its best. Most marvellous of all, however, is the way in which these gall wasps, often closely related species, manipulate the cell chemistry of the oak with their secretions to 'persuade' the tree to create for them galls of such structural diversity.

Fungus experts would probably agree that autumn – the season of fruitfulness in other respects – is also the prime season for their interests. This would apply whether their concern was gastronomic (even the field mushroom is an autumn delicacy) or for the fungi as a group, when they would certainly organize most of their 'fungus forays' – the equivalent of a day's birdwatching or plant hunting – during the autumn months.

Certainly, in our oakwood, autumn is the time to see the greatest range of shapes and colours of these mysterious and often rather insidiously frightening organisms. On a superficial examination, oakwoods as a whole would seem to contain more fungal species than any other habitat, just as they do insect species. In numerical terms this is probably a true reflection of the situation, but most of the oakwood fungi are 'generalists', not too choosy as to habitat. When it comes to groups of fungi recognizably typical only of a certain woodland type, beechwoods, birchwoods and conifers would all easily outscore the oak.

In the leaf litter beneath the oak, year after year, emerges an ideal example of this extraordinary group. Unlike many fungi, this one is as often as not first detected by a really foul, rotting-meat sort of smell. With sufficient determination, the odour can be traced to an upright, cylindrical, greyish-white fungus with a distinct cap, whose scientific name, *Phallus impudicus* (*impudicus* meaning immodest), tells all about its size and shape. Equally appropriate is its colloquial name, stinkhorn. This fungus grows with astonishing speed, rarely taking more than a day and a night, from an underground, white, pea-sized start, through a table-tennis ball stage (called a 'witch's egg'), which emerges through the soil surface and bursts to reveal the bell-shaped, slimy, green cap, which is rapidly propelled 6 or 8 inches (15–20 cm) into the air on a thick, hollow stem. The slimy cap, which produces the smell, contains the spores which are the fungal means of spread. The smell attracts flies in dozens, particularly blue- and green-bottles, so the technique is speedily effective as the flies trample around on both slime and spores. If all goes well, the flies will then land on earth suitable for germination, and the spores they have inadvertently collected will shoot out thread-like hyphae. Some spores approximate to male, others female, and when opposite 'sexes' meet, the hyphae fuse together and form a mycelium whose cells have two nuclei. This mycelium gives rise to the next generation of fruiting bodies, which appear initially as buds on the mycelium and then speedily assume their characteristic shape. Two days later, the original stinkhorn fruiting body has collapsed and is beginning to wither, itself a victim of decomposition and decay.

What are fungi? A group of plants, certainly, but so used are we to plants being predominantly *green*, at least in summer, that the vast array of white and grey fungi, and those of all the other colours of the rainbow, seem for some reason not to qualify as real plants. There may be some justice in this seemingly harsh assessment, for there is a fundamental difference. The green of most plants indicates the presence of chlorophyll, and that, in its turn, means that green plants can create, from water, carbon dioxide and sunlight, their own food supply. So, to a large extent, they are independent organisms, not needing external assistance to survive.

Not so the fungi. They are among the organisms lacking chlorophyll, and thus cannot create their own nourishment. Also unlike the green plants whose cell walls are made of the familiar cellulose, fungal cell walls are made of chitin, the same substance as insects' body walls. Like the members of the animal kingdom, they must live on 'second-hand' food, either as saprophytes feeding on dead organic material, or as parasites on other living organisms. There is a tradition that the living world is divided into the two 'kingdoms' of animals and plants, but some groups become difficult to classify as simply as this: the viruses, for example – are they plants or just highly elaborate chemicals? The fungi, too, have so many strange ways of life that they confused even a taxonomist as revered as Linnaeus, the father of the modern systems of classifying living things. He placed them in the aptly named genus *Chaos*, under the family heading of *Vermes*, or worms.

Our knowledge of even the higher fungi is surprisingly scanty for such a huge gathering of by and large conspicuous organisms – estimated at up to 100,000 named species. Of course, they are only really conspicuous for a few months – very commonly in late summer and autumn – when their fruiting bodies appear above ground. Perhaps this is part of the origin of their early mystery, this sudden springing-up, often startlingly rapid growth, and equally sudden vanishing from the scene. 'Growing like a mushroom', we say. Then, too, there are plenty of stories about fungi, both good and bad; for example, some were the fore-runners of modern drugs (like penicillin), while others were held in awe because of their well-known deadly poisonous effects, and this mystique to some extent continues to the present day. The fruiting period may be conspicuous if short, but beneath the surface (of the soil, or plant tissue, or decaying matter) threads of fungal hyphae ramify through the substrate. The ancient Greeks called fungi '*mykes*' – a word they used for mushroom-shaped objects. The word persists geographically in the old city of Mycenae, but in fungal form as mycelium, the name given to a tangled mat of hyphae.

On the boles of the older, more gnarled oaks through the wood can be seen conspicuous bracket fungi, looking like small shelves, often several inches across. The most remarkable of these in appearance is called the beefsteak fungus because of its uncanny similarity in colour and texture, and feel astonishingly enough, to a piece of fresh raw steak. Beefsteak fungi most commonly occur on oak, but one that in the last couple of years has appeared on our oak – perhaps an indicator of its ripe old age – also occurs on many other deciduous trees. This has no common name, but is called *Ganoderma lucidum*. It is a saprophyte, drawing its energy from decaying parts of

*Beefsteak fungi on oak bole*

the oak trunk. The upper surface is semicircular, and ridged like a giant oyster shell. It is hard, like a pie crust, and a most beautiful purplish-red in colour. The underside is much paler. When it is shedding its spores and the weather is calm, these drift down and cover the shoulders of the roots (as they join the trunk) with a dust that looks just like instant coffee powder.

Another of these bracket fungi, or more properly, polypores, is common in deciduous woodlands on the Continent but has only just made its appearance in Britain. Despite the fact that such fungi usually herald the impending doom of a living tree, or signify the departure of a grand old stump, this one has a fascinating quality that would make it a desirable addition to any woodland scene. It is called *Omphalotus*, with the common name of Jack o' lantern because its large, rather tufty outgrowths give rise, after dark, to a mysterious phosphorescent or luminous glow.

If these fungi cause concern because they indicate that all is not well with the tree on which they are growing, there are others that are far more troublesome to the oak. One is much, much smaller and comes from quite a different family. This is oak mildew, visible in late summer and autumn as a powdery white dusting over the leaves, especially of young Lammas shoots. In severe cases, mildewed shoots are very conspicuous from a distance, and close inspection shows the crumpled appearance of the damaged leaf surface. Damage shows itself in poor acorn crops, much-reduced growth rates, and in the susceptibility of severely afflicted trees to other pests and diseases. Every so often, perhaps two or three times a century, outbreaks of 'decline' or 'die-back' are widely reported from oakwoods. It may be that these in general follow the pattern of one well-studied case history, where early leaves were savagely attacked by tortrix moth caterpillars and their later replacements by a heavy mildew outbreak. The *coup de grâce* may have been given by another fungus, notorious for attacking elderly or injured tree roots, called *Armillaria*.

Where *Armillaria* has struck, be it in woodland, an orchard, or a garden, the result over several years is devastating. Colloquially, *Armillaria* is known as the bootlace fungus because of the bootlace-like nature of its mycelium around the larger roots of its victims, or as honey fungus because of the characteristic colour of the clumps of toadstools ranging from 1 to 6 inches (2.5–15 cm) high that appear at the base of the trunk of an infected tree in autumn, and strike dread into the heart of forester, farmer or gardener.

Although the fungus is supposedly unable to make inroads into healthy tree roots, *Armillaria* fruiting bodies produce thousands of spores from the white gills below the honey-coloured cap, and as there are always dead roots in the soil, a reservoir for infection is ever-present. The mycelium is blackish, with many-branched threads called rhizomorphs, which ramify for

*Death cap*

considerable distances through the soil, invading any dead or damaged roots that they meet. Peeling back the layer of root bark reveals the lethal layer of mycelium, which will eventually penetrate up into the trunk as well. Fortunately, occurrences of this fungus in the oakwood have been few and far between, on isolated trees away from the main stands of timber: long may it remain so.

Other fungi whose fruiting bodies appear beneath the oak are not lethal to plants, but may well be so to unwary humans that try to eat them. One of the more poisonous ones regularly appears under the oak: its name, death cap, is alarming enough, but the problem is that it looks quite field mushroom-like, perhaps an explanation as to why it accounts for most deaths due to fungus poisoning. Like the field mushroom, it is a few inches high, with a yellowish, buffish or brownish cap initially hemispherical, similar to a button mushroom but expanding to a flat parasol 3 or 4 inches (7.5–10 cm) across. Its gills, holding the spores, are white rather than chocolate brown as in the field mushroom. The death cap is *Amanita phalloides*, and a related species, *Amanita virosa*, the destroying angel, is just as poisonous and perhaps, being whiter-capped, even more easily confused with the field mushroom. The destroying angel does not, though, grow on grassy meadows, being a beechwood specialist. Strangely, another couple of *Amanitae*, *A. vaginata* and *A. inaurata*, are edible and, as grisettes, are regarded as a considerable delicacy. They do occasionally occur in the oakwood and are widespread in deciduous woods in general. They are much browner-capped than the poisonous *Amanitae*, but the only safe rule is to regard them as objects of botanical interest on a fungus foray, *not* as potential accompaniment to bacon and eggs!

If the death cap looks innocuous, the other highly poisonous fungus often appearing beneath our oak shouts a warning with its colouration just as effectively as does a wasp! It, too, is an *Amanita*, *A. muscaria*, the fly agaric.

This is the toadstool that any self-respecting and well-set-up gnome in a children's picture book will be sitting on or living in, perhaps not the best way of alerting youngsters to its hazards. Nonetheless, a group of fly agarics under the oak, caught in a shaft of autumn sunlight, are a most beautiful sight. The stem of the fungus is pure white and the cap crimson with a few flecks of white which are the relics of the 'veil' that surrounded it as it burst through the soil. The gills are also white. Almost a complete sphere to start with, the cap opens to an elegantly contoured, flatly conical parasol. The name relates to the effectiveness of fly agaric as an insecticide, which even Linnaeus knew about, but strangely many of those beneath the oak have holes nibbled in them, presumably by slugs, and give a clear demonstration of how what is lethally poisonous to one creature may be quite harmless to another.

The number of really poisonous fungi is probably small relative to the total number of species and, of many, little is known of their edibility or safety. Sadly, the only real test is to eat one, and this is not to be recommended as a trial in any circumstances: 'If in doubt, don't' is the only safe rule. In some cases, for example *Russula*, cooking destroys the cause of the unpleasant effects and bitter taste of the raw fungus, replacing it with a pleasant reminder of crab or other seafoods. In others, like the common ink cap, a tall thin greyish toadstool often found at the edge of the wood, the cooked fungus is quite tasty but causes the most dreadful of stomach upsets in most people if taken with alcoholic drinks: a reaction paralleled in some of the drugs used to 'dry out' alcoholics.

But what of the really poisonous fungi, the lethal death cap and destroying angel? They contain a number of different poisons, some more harmful than others. Of these, phallodin is extremely damaging to human liver cell walls, and amanitin destroys the liver cell nuclei. Protein synthesis is stopped and the kidneys are usually damaged as the entire digestive system is thrown into fatal disarray.

Of course, the vast majority of fungi are not harmful either to man or to plant, they just play their part in the breakdown and decay of organic matter so that it can be re-used. Some can even be considered as beneficial: not just those, like the field mushroom, favoured as a dietary item by man, but more subtly, in liaising with plant roots to enhance the growth of both plant and fungus. This rather special case of symbiosis is the way of life of perhaps the commonest of the autumn fungi beneath the oak (and throughout the oakwood), the penny bun bolete, *Boletus edulis*. As its name implies, it is one of the edible fungi, with a taste described as 'nutty', and is particularly popular as a delicacy in France. As its colloquial name suggests, the full-grown toadstool is roughly similar in size and shape to a nice, brown-capped, oven-baked bread roll or baker's bun, which at the time that the name was given, could still be obtained for a penny! The penny bun bolete is a squat fungus, with white or yellowish gills under its thick domed cap, and with a fat pinkish-brown stalk.

Underground, the mycelium of the boletes forms a complex web over the plant root surface, in some cases with hyphae penetrating into the outer cells of the root. This intermingling of plant and fungus is called a mycorrhizal association. From it the fungus draws out sugars from the plant cell sap, and probably also some minerals. In return, as it were, the plant gets some other minerals that would otherwise be difficult to obtain, and benefits too from a considerably improved uptake of water. The very colourful *Russula*, carmine to deep purple in hue, is another fungus forming a mycorrhizal association with the roots of our oak. This fungus, often 4 inches (10 cm) or more across its concave opened cap, is regarded by many as one of the most delicious when eaten. The gills and stem are pinkish white, but soon turn brown when broken or cut.

Helpful associations are not limited to plants. A downy white fungus called *Pilobolus* is of common occurrence on animal droppings within the wood, particularly favouring those of herbivores like rabbits or deer (or, out in the fields, horses, sheep and the like). The 'deer-pat' is soon covered with white furry mycelium, which quickly becomes ready to fruit. *Pilobolus* is a relatively lowly fungus, and each tiny black spore is borne on a slender upright thread with a swelling at the upper end. This swelling is fluid-filled, and when a shaft of sunlight hits it, it functions as a lens, warms up and literally explodes, projecting the spore some distance – up to a couple of feet away.

For the fungus, this is a neat method of dispersal towards another pile of droppings, but the spore may sometimes carry a passenger. All animals have in their digestive tracts considerable numbers of microscopic nematodes, usually called 'thread-worms' or just 'worms' with an appropriate expression of disgust. Many or most of these are more or less harmless so far as the animal is concerned, and eventually (as eggs or larvae) pass to the outside world in its droppings. Their aim in life is then to get into, or infect, a fresh host, and this is most simply done by waiting, as a contamination, on the vegetation that the host animal is going to eat. Some nematodes have evolved the habit of climbing out of the droppings, up the hyphae and on to the spores of *Pilobolus*, whence they are catapulted out over the surrounding vegetation. This means of spread gives a far wider and more effective dispersal than they could ever have achieved under their own steam, and must dramatically improve their chances of finding a fresh host.

One of the best places to search for autumn fungi is on a fallen tree trunk. Elsewhere in the wood a victim of a gale some years ago is rotting away, almost submerged in places by brambles, nettles and elder bushes taking advantage of the sudden area of well-lit woodland floor available following the fall of the giant oak and its light-excluding canopy. But this is of interest not just for its range of fungal inhabitants: birds, too, are frequent visitors, and this is one of the best areas to sit, tucked almost out of sight in the elders, watching and waiting.

When a tree dies, falls and decays naturally, the composition of the livestock on it changes dramatically. There are no longer any leaves, so the sap-sucking insects are not present. On the other hand, the wood becomes much softer, and there are the saprobic fungi to feed on, so the burrowing larvae of other insects increase. Some of the range of birds that would feed on the living tree and its inhabitants cannot find sufficient food, while others (perhaps with more catholic tastes) continue to flourish. Yet others, specialists in finding food in these circumstances, appear on the scene for the first time.

First of all come the woodpeckers. The great spotted can chisel into thick bark and still-sound timber to reach grubs, even on the trunk. The sparrow-sized lesser spotted must first concentrate on the smaller branches, though as the bark rots away, it too can get to work on the trunk. Other primary feeders include the magpie and the jay, which are among the most alert, sharp-sighted and cautious of birds – the main reason why you should conceal yourself when watching. The feeding technique of these two is less subtle than the woodpeckers': using their bodily strength as well as their beaks, they peel back sheets of bark to get at the grubs, spiders and earwigs sheltering beneath. Squirrels set about the job in much the same way, for they are by no means averse to adding a little animal protein to their largely vegetarian diet, either in winter, or with birds' eggs in summer. None of these searches each piece of bark at all thoroughly, and this is fortunate for the army of 'clearers-up' that come behind. Given such an opportunity, the smaller blue, coal and willow tits – usually feeding in the higher branches of the trees – join their larger and stouter-beaked relative, the great tit, which often feeds at ground level. Our fallen tree is soon alive with tits, all calling excitedly, and the racket may encourage the smallest scavengers of all to come and join in the feast, treecreepers, goldcrests and wrens. So there is food for all, and the messy feeding habits of the larger birds are most helpful to the smaller, weaker ones.

Even the tit flock does not carry out a persistent and thorough search, and surprisingly soon the party has moved noisily on its way, leaving perhaps a wren or a loudly ticking robin in sole possession. It may be that food resources are better conserved by this 'little and often' form of exploitation – obviously there are some benefits in spreading your larder around, especially if timber merchants or foresters are about, dragging off that which they require and burning the remainder!

But the magpie is in danger of being bypassed. Although it is not the most deep-woodland-orientated of the crow family, tending to avoid unbroken forest-type canopies just as much as prairie farmland or open, treeless marshes or moors, it finds the oakwood, with its rides and clearings, well suited to its taste for the woodland edge. Elsewhere, magpies range over pretty well all types of habitat so long as there are some sheltering trees or bushes within reach, but seem to show a preference for scrub and rough farmland with grassy fields, thick hedges and thickets.

'One for sorrow, two for joy,' goes a version of a rhyme centred on the magpie. Our folklore is rich in reference to this bird, but unusually it is involved with both good and evil omens. The origin of this superstition, like many others, is obscure. It may be that its boldly black-and-white plumage and the very long tail, black shot with iridescent greens and purples, and its harsh chattering calls combine to make the magpie one of the most conspicuous – and thus one of the best-known – of our birds and therefore a likely focus for legend. Some old stories suggest that magpie mystique and evil omens stem from the bird going only partly into mourning (a reference to its pied plumage) at the time of the crucifixion. Others suggest that it refused to go into Noah's ark at the time of the great flood, preferring to sit on the roof and cackle derisively as the rest of the world was submerged.

The present-day distribution of magpies has largely been shaped by man. During Victorian times they were commonly shot and trapped, especially in game-rearing areas, where their habit of eating young birds or eggs (of any species that they came across) led almost to their elimination. Even today, the magpie is regularly shot and is often the commonest victim on the gamekeeper's gibbet. The bird's diet is composed primarily of various invertebrate animals – mostly insect larvae and worms – augmented by carrion, cereal seeds, fruit and berries and the occasional unwary small mammal. In short, it is an excellent example of an omnivore, eating whatever can be easily obtained. On the ground, magpies will walk along sedately while searching for food, breaking into a series of bouncing hops when speed is necessary. They extend their hunt for insects by looking for fly maggots in the fleece of sheep, and often seem to use the back of a sheep as a mobile vantage point to look for prey in the grass below.

In the oakwood, they certainly seem to take their toll of the eggs and nestlings of other birds, but to no apparent avail. Certainly the numbers of other birds do not seem to change from year to year for this reason, and a thoughtful analysis would suggest that a predator is unlikely to influence greatly the numbers of its prey; more likely the other way round. From magpies (or indeed sparrowhawks) and their prey in the oakwood to lions and antelopes on the African plains, the rules are the same: prey numbers govern how many predators can be supported. Were it to be the opposite, there would be a real risk that the predators could 'eat themselves out of house and home'; it would be of no benefit to them if they eliminated their food supply.

A magpie's nest is almost as conspicuous as the bird itself – a huge, football-sized, domed construction of thorny twigs built high in a tree. In the oakwood, the several pairs of magpies all gather their nest twigs from an overgrown hawthorn thicket, so dense that many branches have died for lack of light, giving a good supply of building materials. A few years ago, a nest was once built in the oak itself, but more often now it is the tall slender willows in the damper parts of the wood that are favoured.

Over Britain as a whole, despite the adverse pressures exerted by man, the magpie has shown itself well able to adapt to modern life (to say the least!), scavenging for food on town outskirts and rubbish tips and secretively visiting garden bird tables, usually at first light. The legend of the 'thieving magpie' refers to the habit of these birds (and other members of the crow family) of collecting bright objects. Why they do this is difficult to explain – perhaps it is for nest ornamentation, or perhaps the birds are just being inquisitive. Such opportunism (and theft) can pay off: in Manchester magpies have learnt to relate milkmen to the egg-cartons they often deliver, and there are now many angry households where these have been opened, and the contents consumed, early in the morning and right on the doorstep!

Although obviously an important season, for many reasons, to just about every small creature in the oakwood, for the shrews autumn has particular significance. Unlike the other small four-footed-and-furry oakwood creatures, the mice and voles, the two shrews, common and pygmy, eat only animal matter and thus face a particularly testing time during the autumn and winter months, when small food animals either burrow deep (like worms) or overwinter as minute eggs or well-concealed pupae (many insects). Perhaps the most striking feature of shrew population dynamics is that each autumn the adult animals all die off after completing their breeding season, leaving only the young born during the summer to survive over winter and to breed from early spring onwards. It is thought that some of the first young to be born in spring may reach sexual maturity and breed towards the end of the summer, in years when food is plentiful, and they too will attempt to survive the winter to breed again in the next year.

Both species occur in the oakwood, though their identification is not the simple matter that their two names might imply! The common shrew (colloquially called shrew-mouse, or ranny) is widely distributed all over Britain up to an altitude of about 3000 feet (900 m), and occurs in good numbers in most habitats. Numbers are perhaps highest in scrubby grassland, but it is also numerous in deciduous woodland. Typical shrew features are a long conical nose, well appointed with whiskers which are for ever on the twitch, and tiny bead-like and disturbingly expressionless eyes. The fur of the back is velvety, and very dark brown, sometimes near-black, a short summer coat being replaced by an autumn moult to a longer-haired version, in the same colour, giving better thermal protection during the winter. The underparts are paler – often dirty-white or yellowish. Youngsters are perhaps slightly paler than adults.

As its name implies, the pygmy shrew *is* smaller, but as shrews, like humans (and unlike birds), grow considerably from weaning to adulthood, this is a feature to be treated with some caution. Adult pygmy shrews only exceptionally exceed $2\frac{1}{2}$ inches (6 cm) so anything over this length is likely to be a common shrew. As with so many things, experience is the best teacher of the subtleties of identification, which in the shrews are the generally sandier-brown fur of the pygmy and its relatively longer, thicker, and more densely fur-covered tail. Strangely enough, identifying skull remains in owl pellets is almost easier than separating the living animals! In each upper jaw there is a row of five conical, red-edged teeth between the incisors and the molars: in the common shrew these decline steadily in size from front to back, while in the pygmy shrew they are uneven, with the third central one being particularly large.

In the common shrew, two litters, each of up to eight youngsters, seem to be the norm, with in exceptional circumstances (usually abundant food and a fine summer) up to five litters on record. The adult common shrew is about 3 inches (7.5 cm) long, of which about half is tail, and weighs about 7 grams – or $\frac{1}{4}$ ounce. The female gives birth to young weighing about $\frac{1}{2}$ gram – a litter of eight thus amounting to 4 grams or almost sixty per cent of their mother's weight: quite a feat viewed through human eyes, and in biological terms betokening a very efficient energy transfer. Obviously this means that the female must eat voraciously both before the birth (gestation is thought to be a little longer than a fortnight) and until the young are weaned, three weeks or so later. Even so, the young develop relatively slowly and their eyes open only a day or two before they are weaned. The young are born in a ball-shaped loosely woven 'nest' of grass, often at or below soil surface level and always well sheltered.

Though relatively less common in woodland, the pygmy shrew is almost as widely distributed as the common and penetrates further into Arctic regions and reaches higher altitudes – such as the summit of Ben Nevis in Scotland! Despite being a smaller animal, its life-history is very similar to that of the common shrew. Both are extremely noisy creatures and can often be heard rummaging in the leaf litter beneath the oak. Much of a shrew's life is spent in tunnels and runways beneath leaves or at the base of grass clumps, and for small creatures they create a powerfully large rustling as they scamper jerkily but swiftly about.

Not only that, but they are very vocal. While they are exploring and foraging for food within their home ranges, they keep up a continuous, soft, high-pitched twittering, which turns to a shrill, raucous screaming (of amazing volume considering the size of the lungs and voicebox that are producing it) when an intruder is discovered. Often these aggressive shouting matches will result in the intruder turning tail, but fights occur often enough. Except during the actual mating period, or while a female has young, shrews are solitary and apparently (to judge from the noise) excessively bad-tempered. Investigations of marked animals in the past have shown that average distances moved between recaptures range from 25 to 55 yards (25–50 m) for breeding females to 110 yards (100 m) or more for roaming males.

Shrews have high energy demands and little capability to store effective quantities of fat, so they are characterized by a forever-active life-style, feeding busily day and night, winter, spring, summer and autumn alike. It has been found experimentally that pygmy shrews need an intake of between 5 and 10 grams of food each day, which compares astonishingly with their body weight of 3 to 5 grams! Their day (and night) seems to be divided into ten or a dozen periods of feverish food-hunting activity, each separated by a short rest period. For both species, the major food items are various soil and litter invertebrate animals, with beetles, earthworms, grasshoppers, spiders and woodlice predominating. Although their choice is wide, it *is* a choice, as they tend to reject some insect larvae, enchytraeid worms, springtails and millipedes. So there is little indication in their diet of how the two species avoid occasional conflict, sharing a habitat as they do. It seems most likely that their continuously noisy habits may help in this, as it is known that pygmy shrews show a rapid avoidance reaction to the screams of an oncoming common shrew and, although they may scream abuse back, they will never stay to fight!

For deer, autumn is generally regarded as the main rutting season, when the males (bucks or stags) display their strength and indicate their potential sexual prowess to the females (does or hinds) in a series of ritualized displays ranging from depositing droppings in regular spots and debarking trees to the powerful challenging roaring of the red deer stag and the fights that accompany it. Such fights may be ritualized, but as trials of strength they are carried out in earnest and on occasion the death of one of the combatants may result.

Clearly, when oak woodland or forest covered much of the lowland British landscape, there were many more deer, and these were more widely distributed than at present. Today, over much of southern lowland Britain except those areas (like the New Forest in Hampshire or Epping Forest in Essex) where the deer herds are well known, to see a deer in an oakwood is a red-letter event. The situation is further complicated by the difficulty of establishing what is ancestrally wild from the herds (of both native and alien species) that derive from introductions by man or escapes from deer parks.

Although our oakwood normally does not contain deer, on occasion fallow deer visit it from other woods nearby. Despite their size, deer (and particularly the speckle-coated fallow) are well camouflaged and, unless disturbed into a headlong panic, move with astonishing silence through the trees. The usual first sign of their presence is in the soft mud of an oakwood path after a spell of autumn rain: all the deer have two toes on each foot, which is cloven like those of sheep or goats but much more pointed-tipped than either. Not unnaturally, the size of the slots, as the footprints are called, varies with the size of the deer that made them, so some idea of the visitor's identity can be gained straight away. Characteristically, fallow deer slots have a concave 'dent' on each outer surface, distinguishing them from those of the introduced sika, which are convex. Both are larger than the roe deer's and much larger than the tiny slots of the (again introduced) muntjac.

Should the deer itself be seen, it is a tail view that is of most use for identification purposes – fortunate, as often the best sightings will be of a swiftly departing beast! In the north the huge native red deer may enter oakwoods, but over much of Britain, the likely visitors or residents are the fallow, believed by some to have been introduced a very long time ago, and sika, introduced from Japan during the last century to several deer parks from which they subsequently escaped. The smallest deer in Britain, the muntjac from India and China, and the Chinese water-deer, were both originally introduced at Woburn in Bedfordshire at the turn of the century and are now thinly spread over several Midlands and southern counties. The other unarguable native, which falls between these two pairs of species in size, is the roe deer. From behind, fallow and sika have a white 'bottom' surrounding their tails with a dark, roughly semicircular mark separating it from the back. In the case of the sika, the tail too is white, but the fallow has a bold vertical black stripe down the centre of its tail. From behind, the dog-sized muntjac and water-deer show little bottom pattern at all, but the curiously humped back of the muntjac can often easily be seen. The roe deer, intermediate in size and a rich red-brown in colour, has a small, almost circular, white bottom patch with no dark marginal markings.

In the autumn, the male fallow deer head for their traditional woodland rutting sites, usually in mid-October. They have spent the summer apart from the herd of the does and fawns while their new antlers grow (the antlers of the deer family are shed each year, in contrast to the horns of groups like the cows and the antelopes which are permanent fixtures). In a mature buck fallow, the antlers are impressive, with a couple of forward-pointing prongs before the palmate tip is reached. Each of these can best be likened to a giant holly leaf in shape, and further help to separate fallow from sika, whose antlers are narrow and pronged up to the tip.

At the rutting site senior males will mark out a 'territory' by fraying the bark of nearby saplings with their antlers and leaving 'scent-posts' by urinating regularly on the same spots. They also use the pungent excretions of a gland by the eye, which get rubbed off on to the vegetation as the antlers are used to thrash the undergrowth about. For a normally relatively silent animal, the following month is full of roaring challenges, battles, the rounding-up of small herds of does and the attempted 'kidnapping' of does from the harems of nearby bucks. Mating takes place during the autumn with all the does over which the buck has been able to maintain control, and after an eight-month gestation the fawns (sometimes twins) are dropped in deep undergrowth, where they rely on absolute stillness and their dappled coat camouflage to protect them over the first very hazardous weeks.

For the roe deer in oakwoods elsewhere, things are somewhat different. Roe are unusual among the deer in being monogamous, and the rut consists of fraying trees and scraping the ground with the antlers. These are small – about the same length as the deer's head – with two or three prongs. Most characteristic, though, of the roe deer rut is the discovery of well-worn tracks round frayed trees, very often in a figure-of-eight pattern, where the buck and doe have indulged in extended ritualized chases.

The rutting season is earlier for roe than fallow deer, often starting in early August. After mating, the buck may leave the doe until the start of winter, at about which time the embryo that he fertilized some months before begins to develop. This process, called delayed implantation, is one way that evolution has conceived of allowing energy-sapping and important events in an animal's life-cycle to take place at the most advantageous times.

*Fallow deer*

The gestation period for a roe deer, better described in the particular circumstances as a 'developmental period', is about five months. So, without delayed implantation, a fawn conceived in August would be born into the rigours and hazards of the coldest part of the year, but because the fertilized ovum is held back and not implanted in the uterus to begin development until midwinter, the youngster (often twins in roe) arrives into the world in May or June, at a time when there is plenty of undergrowth, plenty of food, and a reasonably warm climate to welcome it.

Although they regularly pass beneath the oak, and during the hot summer evenings pause to rest in its shade, the oakwood foxes have their earth some distance away in a sandy bank beneath the gnarled roots of an extremely old field maple. Just as it does for some of the predominantly flesh- or protein-eating birds, autumn produces dietary changes in the fox, which in this otherwise largely carnivore-free country, we tend to regard as our main predatory mammal. In autumn, however, the fox takes advantage of the various fruits available, and an examination of the droppings (with their characteristic twisted wisp of fur or grass looking like a tail at one end), which are to be found anywhere along the oakwood paths, shows them to be full of pips and stones from the woodland rose hips, blackberries, sloes and wild cherries.

As autumn advances towards winter, the effects of a steadily diminishing food supply will make themselves apparent. The vixen has spent much of the summer raising her cubs, and in some degree training them to hunt for themselves as they accompanied her on excursions through the wood. Any male cubs will probably have ranged away from their home by now, in search of satisfactory territory, but (sadly, in human terms) their inexperience will also have been revealed. Many, or perhaps even most, will be dead or soon to die, victims of hunger, road traffic, guns or snares. The young vixen cubs will soon follow, but they will not go far, often establishing a territory or home range adjacent to their mother's. But many of these, too, will fall victim to winter's hard times.

Save when the vixen is with her cubs, or on heat and with a dog fox, the life of a fox is a solitary one. Mating takes place in midwinter, and by the end of winter the vixen has chosen and suitably modified the earth in which she gives birth to her cubs after an eight-week gestation period. These are often difficult times, as food is usually short. A fox will endure brief periods of severe weather, like snowfall, curled up snug and in shelter, but foxes do not have the advantages of a true hibernation and after a couple of days are forced to resume hunting or turn to any form of carrion, be it eating spoiled apples on a farm rubbish heap, rummaging in dustbins in the nearby village, or scavenging on the local refuse tip. At such times, the fox may even tackle its most difficult and best-protected prey, the hedgehog.

The fox cubs arrive in the world in much the same way as puppies. There are usually between three and five of them, snub-nosed, blunt-eared and pot-bellied. They are born with fur, and with their eyes still tightly closed, but they can nevertheless scramble actively about the den, squeaking hungrily, in search of the vixen and her milk. The vixen stays with the cubs continuously for several days, while the dog fox brings food to her. As spring advances, she leaves them for brief periods and the male's role is reduced: he returns to his own territory nearby for much of the time. All foxes mark their territorial boundaries with their urine at regular spots, these markers telling other foxes not just that they are entering a territory, but also giving details of the sex and physical condition of the occupant.

Early in the summer, the cubs emerge from the earth for brief evening romps, very active and alert, but in a good year plump and still wearing their rather downy cub fur. Obviously as they grow their food demands increase, but during the summer months life becomes much easier for the hunting vixen. There are plenty of earthworms and beetles around at night, and these form a fair proportion of the food supply. In addition, there are the eggs and young of birds nesting on or near the ground, particularly (to the gamekeeper's fury) succulent pheasants. Small mammals, too, feature prominently. There are few sights more delightful than to watch a fox hunting fieldmice or voles. Often enough the vixen will sit upright, silent and tautly alert under the low-hanging branches of the oak, ears and eyes trained on the grassy area just beyond the canopy. As they move through their runways in the tangle of dead grass and other vegetation just above the soil surface, these small rodents often squeak – chattering among themselves – or inevitably make gentle scuffling and rustling noises. Once the vixen's twitching ears have pin-pointed the origin of the sound, she will leap to it. It is this leap that is the real spectacle: cat-like would be one way of describing it but that is hardly adequate. With nose and ears trained on target like a pointer hunting dog, she springs clear of the ground in a graceful semicircle, bushy tail streaming out behind, to land 3 or 4 feet (90–120 cm) away, front paws first and close together, hopefully right on top of her prey. The rodent in this difficult terrain may wriggle free, but another pounce follows, and another, until the front feet can let the teeth take over.

The other large mammalian predator that frequents the oakwood, the badger, is normally considered to be much more of an omnivore year-round than the fox. There are, though, similarities in their autumn diet that reflect the generally increasing scarcity of food. Foxes are lithe and active and can stretch or leap for hanging fruit; not so the rotund heavyweight badger, which will forage on fallen fruit or dig for edibly juicy roots. The badgers' set is away down in the distant corner of the oakwood, a huge domed mound perhaps 10 yards (9 m) across and with several entrances. As you get closer to it, so the many vague paths that have been barely discernible in the vegetation become more obvious and turn into well-trodden tracks, for badgers are creatures of habit. Another good sign of the proximity of badger habitation is the discovery of a dung pit, or latrine, for in defecating too these creatures habitually use small holes that they have dug for the purpose a few yards away from the set.

The home life of the badger is very different from that of the fox. Although badgers often hunt on their own (except for sows with well-grown cubs) they are altogether more social animals than are foxes. The set will contain a series of branching tunnels, many ending in a living chamber, and although each animal will have a 'room' to itself, several badgers, old and young, male and female, will share the set throughout the year. Obviously the dominant boar and the older sows will exert their power and influence to obtain the quarters they choose, and if a group grows over the years, extensions are excavated to the set.

In autumn the badgers will be feeding as hard and as fast as they can. Unlike the fox, they can accumulate very considerable fat stores beneath the skin and around various internal organs like the kidneys, and this stored fat will help tide them over the lean days of winter when they sleep, breathing shallowly to minimize expenditure of their valuable energy supply. Like some members of the deer family, and seals, delayed implantation of the fertilized egg, or embryo, is a feature of the badger's reproductive cycle. The embryos, fertilized way back at the start of spring, have been floating around loose in the sow's uterus since then. In autumn, hormonal changes cause the embryos to implant – to merge, as a placenta forms, with the uterus wall.

## AUTUMN

This means that the sow
badger must have sufficient
reserves, or feeding periods outdoors,
to support her as the embryos grow,
and this is during the shortest, darkest and coldest
days of winter. Often enough, mild spells and
unfrozen ground will allow her to find succulent
roots or hunt out small mammals hibernating in
the undergrowth, and these foods will be a great
asset, as she gives birth in late January or February
to a litter of up to four cubs. As an additional comfort
and aid to insulation, badgers line their chambers with
dry grass or bracken. This, on any warm winter day,
they will drag out for an airing at the mouth of
the set, but once the young are born the need to air the
bedding increases and it is replaced whenever
possible. With their communal life-style, there may
be several families of young in the set at this time.

*Badgers*

For a few days the sow stays with the cubs, moving very little, but eventually she has to replenish her reserves and, especially on mild nights in late winter when earthworms may be on the surface, she departs to forage. She usually makes sure that the resident boars are out first, however, because given a sufficient hunger drive they may fancy her youngsters as a snack. At this time, too, the female comes on heat, so the boar will be anxious to make contact with her. Her scent marks and her presence deter him from entering her chamber, so he calls her out with a strange high-pitched purring. If she is in season, she responds, and mating may take place on several nights. At this time of year that corner of the oakwood is full of strange noises at night, with puppy-like yelps from the young and growls, purring and often bouts of really harsh screaming (of unknown significance) from the boars and sows.

As summer approaches and the oak leafs out, so the badger cubs emerge at the set entrances each evening for a boisterous communal playtime. This rollicking gambol is (rather prosaically) regarded by animal behaviour students as the time that the young badgers learn a few skills, try their strength, and sort out who is who in the hierarchy: who is dominant, who subservient. From May onwards the young will follow the sow on foraging expeditions, learning by example how to catch worms, dig for roots (and even wasps' nests) and which plants are usefully edible, which not. By now they will be weaned, and soon able to face the world alone. But in the oakwood, summer is a difficult and testing time for young and adult badger alike. In a hot year, the ground is rock-hard and difficult to dig, roots are shrivelled, worms buried deep and the fruit and seed crop yet to appear in any quantity. At this time in a dry year, many of the badgers will desert the oakwood at night, scavenging in the gardens of the village or eating ripening oats, barley or winter wheat in the fields nearby – to the displeasure of the farmer, as each animal flattens a considerable area of standing corn.

Featuring quite prominently in the diet of all the predators that use the oak and the oakwood in general – the owls, the fox and to a lesser extent the badger, and weasels and stoats particularly – are the small rodents. This term is often loosely, and wrongly, applied also to the two shrews, which feature in some predator diets but not in others, where apparently they are found to be distasteful. The true small rodents are the bank vole, the short-tailed vole, and the two fieldmice, long-tailed and yellow-necked.

By far the commoner of the two voles, appearing frequently under the oak (and climbing around in it on occasion) is the bank vole, which is a rich chestnut brown above, with the typical plumply rounded face and furry ears of a vole (as distinct from the pointed nose of a mouse). The tail, also furry, is about half the length of the head and body combined. The short-

*Short-tailed vole*

tailed vole is an irregular visitor to the wood, coming to the oak particularly in autumn when its numbers, which fluctuate very considerably from year to year, are high in the fields surrounding the oakwood. It is much the same 'mouse-size' as the bank vole, but its coat is a drabber undistinguished brown, and its tail only a quarter to a third of the head-plus-body length. Because of its more open normal habitat, the short-tailed vole is largely nocturnal in its activities, resting up in hiding during the day. Remains of both species do feature in the pellets from all the oakwood owls, where they can be separated because bank voles have teeth with roots (rather like ours) and short-tailed have open-rooted, continuously growing teeth (like those of a sheep). Perhaps these dental differences are related to the animals' diets, because the bank vole eats much more soft and succulent greenery and fruit, augmented by nuts and the like in autumn and winter, while tough and abrasive grass stems feature prominently in the diet of the short-tailed, demanding longer-life teeth.

At any time of the year, but perhaps best during the autumn months, a quiet session spent sitting with your back against the trunk of the oak will soon reveal rustlings in the leaf-litter, and these in turn will quickly be traced to a busy bank vole, scurrying around collecting food. Attractively, they rarely take any notice of a silent and reasonably immobile bystander, going about their obviously urgent business unconcerned. In autumn some adults will still be feeding their young in the 'nest', a ball of bark, moss and grasses either underground or in a cleft in a stump. This will be the end of a long breeding season, starting in April, in which four or five litters, on average each of four youngsters, may have been reared. It seems that most of those voles that survive the winter have never bred before the oncoming spring. The first litter grows quickly, being weaned in just over a fortnight and becoming sexually mature after a month or so. This first litter also breeds during the summer, but apparently most other litters produced during the year grow and mature more slowly, and it is these that form the overwintering population.

Winter is obviously the toughest time of year for the bank voles, and they need to spend most of their time foraging for food, which becomes scarcer as winter progresses. Not only is starvation a major hazard for them, but bad weather and food shortage inevitably make them less careful as they seek nourishment, this unwariness increasing greatly the chances of their being caught by a weasel or an owl, equally hard-pressed and anxious for a meal. Their diet throughout the year is widely varied, featuring small worms, snails, insects and their larvae, as well as green plants, seeds and fruit. In autumn, two features are particularly attractive to the watcher: to see them using their very considerable climbing agility to reach ripe blackberries, and to observe them struggling back home with an acorn, sweet chestnut or hazel nut held in their teeth. With so large a load, they have to hold their heads high and back, and in consequence have difficulty in seeing where they are going, blundering along with often comical results.

Bank voles handle nuts, especially hazel nuts, in a distinctive way, holding them on the ground with the forefeet and gnawing off the 'pointed' end, which is uppermost. Squirrels also hold the nuts in their forefeet, though off the ground, and gnaw a small part from the pointed end then insert their long incisor teeth as a lever and split the nutshell open from top to bottom. The fieldmice tackle nuts in a similarly characteristic way, holding them down with their forefeet, positioned with the nut's long axis from side to side, and gnawing a large hole in the centre of the nutshell to reach the nutritious kernel within. Thus the discarded nutshells found on the oakwood floor can tell us which animal has eaten them.

When full grown, fieldmice are larger than voles, and have pointed muzzles always on the twitch, huge almost circular ears, and very long, almost naked tails. There are two species in Britain, and they are none too easy to distinguish. Both are 'mouse-brown' above and white below, the border between the two being of yellowish fur. In the long-tailed fieldmouse (or woodmouse), there is a tiny yellowish-brown patch of fur on the chest, which in the rather larger yellow-necked mouse extends upwards to produce a yellowish collar – hence its name. So difficult are they to separate that the distribution of the two is not all that well known, save that the long-tailed seems pretty well universal in Britain, and is the one we see beneath the oak, while the yellow-necked seems to be confined to southern England.

Once again, in autumn, sitting at the base of the oak is a good place for fieldmouse watching. They are out in the open more often even than bank voles, but are decidedly more nocturnal, so autumn and winter evenings with failing light are best. Apart from differences in colour, tail length and head shape, fieldmice also move in quite a different way from voles. Though they too scurry, they are very, very fast and intersperse their scurrying with occasional jumps, rather like the clockwork mice children are given for Christmas and just as erratic. Autumn is also the best period to see fieldmice because their numbers are then at their highest. Strangely, for our most common and widely distributed small mammal, there are still many gaps in our knowledge of fieldmouse ecology and behaviour. These high numbers all attempt to overwinter, feeding on seeds ranging in size from grass seeds to the acorns off the oak – and in the wood, the acorn crop is obviously crucial for many of the fieldmice. Autumn nights are spent feeding and storing any surplus in the old nest against the colder days of winter, although many females may still be tending litters. Winter survival depends on both the severity of the weather and on the quantity of seed produced by all sorts of plants the previous summer. In early spring, the successful survivors start to breed, but at this time conditions are at their toughest. Seed stocks are at their lowest, and no fresh seed has yet appeared, so the diet of the average fieldmouse now includes many more beetles, snails (which they nibble their way into just like nuts), caterpillars and the like.

The fieldmouse population is at its lowest ebb in early summer, and mortality is high, but as summer progresses and more food becomes available, things improve. Survivors from early litters may breed in their first year, but other young must survive over winter before their turn comes. The reproductive cycle is carried out at a slower pace than in the voles, with gestation taking almost a month and raising the young to weaning three weeks or so. Litters generally average five or six young, and the number of litters each female produces, although not known precisely, is bound to be less than those of a female vole. Despite the hazards, and despite their many predators, fieldmice survive well in the wood, to delight us with their tree-climbing ability (they even rob eggs from the tits' nests), their liking for acorns and their short-sightedly eccentric progress under the oak.

Artistically, autumn is the season of golds, rusts and browns. Pursuing this line of thought brings into sharper focus than usual two of the oak's inconspicuous but regular visitors throughout the year, both 'little brown jobs' in birdwatching parlance, the dunnock and the wren. In these circumstances, the dunnock's name is most appropriate: it derives from the Old English 'dun' – an indeterminate sort of brown – and 'ock', meaning 'little'. Dun is a harsh description of the bird's plumage: breast, throat and face are an unusual leaden grey, while the back is a mixture of browns, chestnut and black.

The dunnock is often called the hedge sparrow, but misleadingly, as a closer view will show a needle-fine, insect-eating beak very different from the squat, seed-crushing wedge-shaped beak of the house sparrow, to which the dunnock is not related. Its tweed-like plumage comes into its own during the breeding season. Dunnocks build neat grass and moss nests, hair-lined, and usually low in brambles, shrubs or hedges. Before the bushes leaf out, camouflage is at a premium, and few birds are less visible, crouched low in a nest of old brown grass, than the hen dunnock. She sits very tight, no twitch of tail or flicker of eyelid betraying her position. Once she has been disturbed, though, the clutch of eggs her departure reveals seem the antithesis of camouflage, as they are bright blue, unspeckled, and stand out glaringly against their sombre background.

Another colloquial name for this bird – hedge Betty – gives an indication of its endearing nature. It always seems active, even fussy, in its feeding as it hops along deep under the bushes picking up such minute food items that even binoculars cannot help to identify. Rarely does it seem flustered by nearby humans, and goes about its business as if we did not exist. In spring, the birdwatcher under the oak may find himself or herself in the centre as male dances round female, wings and tail flicking almost in a frenzy, and there will be short, excited chases punctuated by bursts of song. This is tuneful and cheerful, if slightly scratchy, and ends in mid-stream, almost with a question mark.

Such an ending is appropriate, for despite the opportunity for close observation we still know surprisingly little about this enigmatic bird. Its social behaviour and diet are poorly understood, as is the reason for the occasional evening chorus of shrill piping dunnock alarm calls, occurring even when no predators are about. Sometimes the oakwood on an autumn evening will appear *full* of dunnocks – each only a few yards from its neighbour, and each piping loudly. Most dunnocks are decidedly stay-at-home – ringing recoveries indicate a sedentary existence. But every few years there is evidence of considerable autumn migration and large numbers appear at coastal bird observatories. Why? And why should this tame and approachable woodland – and garden — bird in Britain be translated into an extremely shy denizen of deepest cover, rarely seen, on the Continent, even in those countries where small-bird persecution is not the rule?

If the dunnock is normally demure and self-effacing, the other 'little brown job' from the oak could hardly be more brash. Although almost the smallest of British birds (only the goldcrest and firecrest are smaller), the wren is surely the most cheerfully vocal. Given the slightest suggestion of a fine day, autumn, winter, spring or summer, wrens are in song, their machine-gun-like bursts of tuneful ebullience astonishingly loud for such small creatures. Often, even when the summer dawn chorus is at its peak, careful listening will reveal that the wren is one of the prime songsters.

The wren is deservedly among the most popular of our birds. Back in the days before decimal currency and galloping inflation, it featured – tail as always perkily cocked – on the reverse of our smallest coin, the farthing, the only bird to be honoured in this way. Perhaps its popularity stems from its presence year-round in almost all habitats – not just the oakwoods, but even sea cliffs and dense reed beds, as well as farmland and gardens. Wrens spend a great deal of time busily scurrying and scuffling among the leaves beneath the oak and on its rugged bark, or in the ivy, seeking out insects and spiders with their needle-fine beaks.

Strangely enough, British bird-protection laws owe much to the wren. The race of wrens from the remote island of St Kilda, 60 miles (95 km) out in the Atlantic west of the Hebrides, are clearly distinct from their mainland counterparts, being larger and greyer. Such was the mania for nest and egg collecting in Victorian times that this island race (with a total population of only a couple of hundred pairs) was threatened with extinction at the hands of St Kildans, supplying the demands of Victorian gentlefolk. Once the threat was appreciated, conservationists mounted tremendous pressure in Parliament to give legal protection to the St Kilda wren, and from this small beginning, and insignificant but noisy bird, arose modern bird-protection legislation.

In cold weather, wrens tend to gather together in sheltered spots to roost overnight, like the old green woodpecker nest in the broken-off branch on the oak. Sometimes these huddles contain amazing numbers, and once sixty were reported emerging from a nestbox after one cold winter night, a figure putting the boy-scouts-in-phone-box records to shame! In spite of these communal roosts and the warmth they generate, wrens are very susceptible to the hardships imposed by bad winter weather, and many may die in prolonged snowfall. In the severe winter of 1962–3, an estimated seventy to eighty per cent of our wren population perished from cold. This story had a happy ending, though, as numbers were back to normal in most areas within three years. Since then, the population has continued to grow to the extent that the wren may now be one of the most numerous as well as widespread birds.

Obviously this implies that, given the right conditions, wrens are highly successful breeding birds. The domed nest is compact and well-camouflaged, made of dry leaves and grasses, and usually embedded in a crevice, or deep in ivy, or even under an arching root of the oak if it protrudes a sufficient distance above the soil. The entrance hole is to one side. The male usually constructs several nests, the female eventually choosing one, to which they then add a feather lining. There are usually two or three broods, often of six or more youngsters, in each summer.

This sort of 'productivity' is certainly not matched by another brown, well-camouflaged bird that uses the oak throughout the year. The epithet 'little' certainly does not apply either, but noisy it certainly is, particularly during the autumn. The tawny owl, the subject of these comments, is a comfortable-looking bird, dumpy-bodied and round-headed, its plumage usually a mixture of browns and chestnuts as its alternative name, brown owl, suggests. Through the ages, owls have fascinated man: no wizard would be without one as a familiar, and from ancient Egypt and Greek mythology down to *Winnie the Pooh* of the present day, literary references to owls abound, most associated with their legendary wisdom. This is the most widespread and most numerous of the British owls, and despite the spine-chilling quality of its quavering 'whoo-hoo-hoo' call, it is well-known and well-liked, unusual for a nocturnal creature far more often heard than seen by man.

The tawny owls breed elsewhere in the oakwood, but the oak is often the centre of their activities. Early in the year the male uses it as his major

*Tawny owl*

song-post, during the summer it is a regular feeding station for the young, where they know they can meet a parent bird returning with food, and now, in the autumn, it is the scene of noisy pitched 'battles' as the old male tawny endeavours to chase the young of the year out of his territory.

Tawny owls start their breeding season early. In *Love's Labour's Lost* Shakespeare wrote of their activity:

> When icicles hang by the wall,
> And Dick the shepherd blows his nail,
> And Tom bears logs into the hall,
> And milk comes frozen home in pail,
> When blood is nipped and ways be foul,
> Then nightly sings the staring owl –
> Tu who;
> Tu wit tu whoo, a merry note . . .

Hooting may start before Christmas, and often reaches a crescendo in February as the final squabbles over territorial boundaries are settled. The nest will be in a hollow tree or deserted building: the poet Gray refers in his *Elegy* to 'yonder ivy-mantled tower', in which 'the moping owl doth to the moon complain'.

Tawny owls seem able to gauge with accuracy the availability of food in the coming summer (mostly small rodents of one sort or another, but including worms, birds, fish and frogs) and lay an appropriate number of eggs. None is produced, or just one or two, if food is scarce, but up to ten if it is plentiful. The female starts incubating as soon as the first egg is laid, so (unlike most birds) the young hatch at intervals of roughly two days. In consequence there is a considerable size disparity between the oldest and the youngest chick: should the owls suddenly fall on hard times, the largest will eat the smallest, then the next smallest . . . Although apparently savage cannibalism, this behaviour does give the family the best chance of producing one or two healthy chicks, rather than all the young perishing from starvation. Unusually for British birds, the young tawnies may be dependent on their parents for several months while they learn to fend for themselves. Not until autumn do their parents get fed up and chase them out of the territory, so right through the summer months hungry 'ku-weks' penetrate the woodland night as owlets let their parents know where they are.

Despite their often noisy behaviour at other times, owls hunt on silent wings. Their feathers have a velvety surface and the leading edge of the wing a comb-like fringe so that they do not swish through the air as they swoop with outstretched talons on to their prey. An alternative technique is to sit quietly in the oak, feathers blending in good camouflage with the trunk, and wait for the next meal to scamper along the ground below. The attack is then vertical, with wings held cupped like a parachute, and the kill swift and sure, as needle-sharp talons almost 1 inch (25 mm) long pierce the vital organs of the prey held in a powerfully remorseless grip.

Away across the wood, the little owl family have at long last fledged from their nest, which is situated in an old stubby lightning-blasted oak, as it is in most years. Perhaps because they are much more active during the day and evening, and not so much during the night, little and tawny do not seem often to come into conflict. The little owl youngsters are painfully conspicuous during the day, each perching in different trees, and each surrrounded by a frenzied gathering of scolding small birds. This furore makes them easy to locate, and as they are approached it is only too obvious that they still have much to learn in the way of fear of man, for they sit, glaring boldly at the intruder with bright yellow eyes, 'clicking' in an irascible manner and bobbing their heads up and down. The bits and pieces of fluffy down still sticking to their heads and facial discs give this stern demonstration of annoyance more of an air of farce! Each year when the young have left the nest, a check through the residual contents (by now revoltingly smelly) gives an idea of the range of their diet, for although they feed largely on worms and beetles, they do take birds, and occasionally the mortal remains of some may be found, like starlings, song thrushes or, most surprisingly, even a mistle thrush, and an adult at that. There cannot be much of a size difference between the little owl and the mistle thrush – and the latter is among the boldest when it comes to seeing off marauding magpies, jays, owls and hawks. Unless the thrush is taken by surprise, its capture must be a battle royal but, weight for weight, the little owl is one of the most powerful of avian hunters. It tends to hunt by sitting motionless on a branch of the oak overlooking a more or less open area, and when prey passes beneath it 'parachutes' down on top of it, striking with its talons – perhaps this is the way of the mistle thrush's end.

The other major flying predator in the oakwood hunts its prey in a much more active way. This is the sparrowhawk, as its name implies something of a specialist bird eater, though as it is often a predominantly woodland hunter sparrows feature relatively infrequently in its diet. Over the last two centuries, few birds have suffered so much at the hands of man: first it was gamekeepers, destroying the sparrowhawk as 'vermin'; then egg collectors and taxidermists wreaking havoc; and latterly, over perhaps the last thirty years, pesticides used by farmers have taken a terrible toll. Happily now gamekeepers are fewer in number and better informed, and collectors too are much reduced in numbers, though astonishingly their gruesome hobby

*Sparrowhawk*

still survives 'underground'.

Public opinion and safety legislation have combined to ensure that the ecological impact of pesticides, properly used, is now minimal, a great change from post-war days when the insecticide DDT (and other chlorinated hydrocarbons like it) were hailed as saviours because they were so cheap and so widely effective. In parts of the world where malaria was endemic, human saviour DDT certainly was, but at a high ecological cost. Unknown at the time, the insecticide had the ability to persist and accumulate in the environment from year to year, including being stored in the body fats particularly of predators (because they received many small 'doses' from each item of prey). Ultimately it reached concentrations at which it severely interfered with both breeding behaviour and eggshell thickness, causing many breeding failures and a collapse of the sparrowhawk population, among others.

In the last decade the tide has turned for the sparrowhawk, once again a common woodland bird in the west and north and at long last increasing too in the south and east of England. In the oakwood, it has not nested in the oak itself, at least in recent years, but will probably eventually do so, perhaps choosing an old squirrel's dray or crow's nest for this, but quite happy with a (very untidy) purpose-built one if needs be. As in many birds of prey, there is a considerable size difference between male and female: he is the size of a turtle dove, she often as big as a woodpigeon. Not unnaturally, this influences the size of the birds that they hunt, the male with his chestnut underparts, called a 'musket' by falconers admiring his agile prowess, going for tits and finches, the female capable of tackling thrushes and even pigeons and doves.

Evolution has shaped them well for effective woodland hunting, and to see them rushing through the oak canopies is a real thrill. Unlike the long-winged falcons, built for sheer speed to fly down their prey in direct pursuit, the hawks have short, rounded wings which, with a long tail, give them tremendous manoeuvrability as they dart through the branches following every twist and turn of their intended victim.

With a growing family to feed, often of four or more youngsters, the male can be hard pressed keeping up an adequate supply of food, but again evolution has taken a hand. While the male copes with the demands of the small young, the female hardly leaves the nest. Obviously she is 'on guard', tearing up the food the male brings and passing it to the young in delicate morsels, as well as brooding them, but at the same time she is moulting, so when they are larger and the male is beginning to be harassed by the efforts of hunting, she can take over, with brand-new wing feathers and, of course, the ability to catch considerably bigger and more meaty prey. Watching sparrowhawks hunt, it becomes obvious why so many birds of prey – falcons, hawks, harriers and owls – have such relatively long legs: if you are making a mid-air capture (or, indeed, a terrestrial pounce) you need to be able to keep beating your wings meanwhile – hence the benefits of legs capable of a long stretch.

Autumn, with the gathering of birds like tits into flocks, and the formation of night-time roosts, could be regarded as an easy time for sparrowhawks. But the young need all the food, and particularly catching experience, they can get for, with no doubt at all, times will get harder, the days shorter and prey scarcer as winter develops.

*Fly agaric*

# Index

Page numbers in *italic* refer to illustrations